PRAYER FOR MY CHILD

PRAYER
FOR MY
CHILD

A GUIDE FOR THE PRECIOUS PRAYER OF PARENTS

TIM A. SPILMAN

PICTURES OF LIFE
PUBLISHERS™

Cover and book design, illustrations, etc.: Tim Spilman
Photography: Tim and Stephanie Spilman
Editorial consultant and contributor: Stephanie Keith Spilman

ISBN: 0-9674948-0-X

Manufactured in the United States of America.

PICTURES OF LIFE
PUBLISHERS™
P. O. Box 3235
Holiday, Florida 34690
E-mail: picturesoflife@aol.com

To our children,
Keith, Melissa, Teresa, and Christopher
with love, joy, hope and prayer

"I have no greater joy than this,
to hear of my children walking in the truth."
(3 John 4)

and in memory of
Diana Marie Spilman,
the sister whom I have not yet met

PRAYER FOR MY CHILD

CONTENTS

PART ONE

THE PRAYER FOR MY CHILD GUIDE

A Note from Stephanie...

Dear Tim,

I'm so glad that you're finally getting the Prayer Guide down on paper where other people besides me can benefit from it. Of course, I've heard how your thinking has developed as you've paced the floor for years, but other folks are going to want to know why the items are there — what Scripture has informed your thinking? Does it matter if we have a plan like this, or are we taking this all too seriously? The "lite" version is supposed to be better, after all! Right? But prayer for our precious children isn't dessert, it's the main course, and if it takes more effort to prepare, it is ultimately more satisfying and beneficial, and definitely worth it!

Love, Stephanie

Stephanie,

I'm glad, too, because I need this prayer guide! It's hard for a pastor to admit this, but I'm weak! This was written first for me. Meaningful, purposeful, consistent, passionate prayer is a real struggle for every home, and no less in ours. I appreciate your help as we endeavor to keep it going.

Why is such a complete guide for prayer necessary? My growing conviction is that we parents need (and want) something more substantial than, "Help me, Obi-Wan Kenobi. You're my only hope!"

Are we willing to stretch, for the sake of our beloved children? Are we willing to venture beyond our comfort zone, and give up the idea that the Christian life should always be easy and feel comfortable? Are we willing to go all out in attaining our goal, all the while looking in faith to God for His powerful grace?

May God give us His grace as we tackle this most important and joyful responsibility, prayer for our children!

Love, Tim

PRAYER FOR MY CHILD

INTRODUCTION

What is "PRAYER FOR MY CHILD" all about? It is simply *a prayer guide designed to help Christian parents in establishing and maintaining the effective and consistent practice of covering their children with prayer.* This book includes the PRAYER FOR MY CHILD guide, along with an explanation of the guide's contents, and tips and tools for its use. The guide itself consists of a one-page summary prayer list covering eight main areas of prayer.

Why do I need this guide? *You* may *not* need it, if you already have a systematic, consistent method of praying for your children. But the sad truth is that most Christian parents, even those with the best of intentions, do not have a *serious, purposeful, thorough* approach to this duty of prayer for their children. Seeing that the responsibility of prayer for our children is arguably the most fundamental and important single aspect of Christian parenting, the thought of falling short in its practice should be a troubling one for us all.

The PRAYER FOR MY CHILD system is born out of this father's conviction about the importance of prayer, combined with the frustration and guilt that I have felt about my inadequate practice of this duty on behalf of my four children. Perhaps you, too, like this convicted, frustrated father, sense a need to "get your act together" by devoting yourself to an organized, thorough approach to this eternally important responsibility in your life.

Why do we need a *systematic* approach to this spiritual duty? We need a systematic approach simply because we are by nature so inconsistent and erratic in spiritual duties, and so prone to be ruled by what we are thinking or feeling at the moment rather than by spiritual priorities. It is so easy to fall into the practice of offering much prayer for some needs, especially the more temporally urgent needs, while neglecting or overlooking other matters of *eternal* importance. So many parents, to the spiritual loss of the children they love so dearly, give disproportionate attention to matters of less significance (such as physical needs, or temporal happiness or comfort or success), compared with the attention and effort they devote to the infinitely more weighty matters pertaining to the spiritual and eternal health and well-being of their children. Unless you have a plan, or a systematic approach, you will likely be guided by whatever seems urgent *right now*, while losing touch with your primary focus and true priorities in your prayers. If we are to "cover all the bases," adequately address all areas in which our children are in need, and offer prayer for each need in proportion to the relative spiritual importance of that area of need, we must have a systematic approach to our prayer.

If we *really* believe that God is a God who answers prayer (*He is*; Psalm 65:2, "O you who hear prayer"), and that neglecting prayer for particular needs of our children, for all intents and purposes, amounts to a forfeiture of God's promised provisions for those needs (*it does*; James 4:2, "You do not have because you do not ask"), then we can see that it is a fearful thing to approach prayer in a haphazard or casual manner. So, this *systematic* approach is commended.

What is the approach of *this book* to the PRAYER FOR MY CHILD guide? In this book, the prayer guide is introduced and accompanied by an explanation and implementation

12

plan. The explanation is arranged so that parents can master this prayer guide's content in daily, "bite-sized" increments. Each day, during the parent's *Meeting Time with God* ("daily devotions"), one aspect of the prayer guide's content is considered and prayed about. Then, the content of the teaching is meditated upon and prayed whenever possible throughout the day. The daily increments are designed to be covered in weekly groupings, with Monday through Saturday being days set aside for considering the various aspects of the prayer guide, and Sunday being a day devoted to celebrating God as the focus and end of all our prayers, and resting in His grace and power. In this approach, the guide's contents are covered in a three-week period of time.

What is included in this book? PART ONE of this book contains the prayer guide and the daily explanation of its various elements. At the end of each week's studies, you will find a two-page "THE WORD" worksheet, which is designed to assist you as you focus on particular Scripture passages, identify prayer requests, and keep track of other teachings in your life during the week. This is followed by a SUMMARY PAGE for the week, which includes questions for reflection and space for developing an action plan. After the first week, a **Parental Covenant to Pray For My Children** is included to allow the parent to "officially" commit himself to the joyful task of prayer for his children.

PART TWO of this book contains two valuable resources to assist the parent in arriving at a working evaluation of the child for whom he will pray. These worksheets, the SPIRITUAL INVENTORY WORKSHEET and the SPIRITUAL PROGRESS EVALUATION WORKSHEET, are designed to enable the parent to offer prayers that are relevant to his child's particular, personal needs and situation. These tools will be introduced and explained later.

Several different copies of the PRAYER FOR MY CHILD guide are included in this book. In addition to the copy of the list on page fifteen, another copy of the full list is included at the end of the book for use by the parent in the years ahead. Also, a half-sized copy of the list is provided for posting in a conspicuous place as a daily reminder to pray. Two copies of an abbreviated version on bookmarks are also included. Finally, two copies of a smaller, wallet-sized, abbreviated form of the prayer list are provided. This smaller version is the perfect size for carrying in the parent's wallet or purse. The different versions of this prayer sheet are included to make it easier for parents to keep this duty of prayer ever before them throughout the day.

What is the meaning and significance of the *symbols* used on the PRAYER FOR MY CHILD **guide?** The graphics used on the prayer guide are designed to remind us of our proper focus. The cloud graphic stands for the personal presence and power of God. It is not a picture of God as He is in Himself, but is rather a symbol of God's *hiddenness from our sight* (we cannot see through a cloud) as well as His *accessibility to us* (the cloud, which separates God from us, is a vapory, light, penetrable substance, rather than a dense, thick, impenetrable wall). The round circle around the cloud is meant to be a kind of "window," reminding us that prayer is, as it were, the means to penetrate the cloud that hides God from us, and to gain access into the "other world," into His spiritual presence. The father holding his child is meant to be a picture of the function of prayer, in that we "carry" our child in the arms of faith into the presence of God to receive His care and blessing, as we would carry our child in our physical arms to the doctor. The man is facing toward the cloud, to signify that the eyes of faith are always on God as the goal of our faith and the delight of our souls.

What will be the goal of my prayer as I am guided by this PRAYER FOR MY CHILD **guide?** This is the all-important question. We should all agree that the goal of our prayer for our children is their happiness. When we determine what will make our children happy, then the priority of our prayer for them will be clear. Of course, the ultimate goal of everything we do for our children is that they would live to God's glory forever. But to glorify God means to seek and find our happiness *in Him.* In glorifying God, we value and cherish Him above everything. No matter what earthly and temporal benefits our children receive, they will miss happiness unless they have God. If we have decisively determined that our children's happiness is tied to God, then our prayers on behalf of our children will focus on God and obtaining for them an eternal relationship with Him.

Therefore, are your prayers going to be *GOD*-CENTERED or *THIS-WORLD*-CENTERED? Is your greatest desire for your child and the greatest need that you recognize for his happiness, *"Show me Your glory!"* (Exodus 33:18)? Or, is it something else? We need to determine at the outset that God Himself, and God alone, will bring happiness to our child, and then set out to establish the priority in all our prayers accordingly.

Consider the parent's joy to which faithful devotion to the duty of prayer leads. We must see *our own* joy as part of the goal in praying, as we find joy in the true happiness of the ones we love so much. As the apostle says in 3 John 4, our *highest* level of joy is attained when the children committed to our care are "walking in the truth."

What is the place of prayer in child rearing? Prayer is at the *beginning* of child rearing. The reason we must begin with prayer is because prayer is the means through which God's power, the power of His grace, flows into our children's hearts and lives. Apart from this grace, all of our efforts are in vain. Many parents observe wayward, ungodly children from other families, children who have made a shipwreck of their faith, and say, *"That would never happen to my children. I'm too good and faithful a parent for that. I teach my children, and correct them, and make sure our home environment is well-organized and disciplined."* This is a dangerous attitude. Why? It is not because teaching and disciplining and organization aren't important; they obviously are crucial. It is rather dangerous because, when we are *trusting in the means* of child rearing, the *methods,* and the *human effort,* rather than God and His grace, our efforts will be *in vain.* We parents are the providers for our children, but the *one thing* they need more than anything else (God, and a relationship of love with Him) is something that we are powerless to give them! God must grant them His Spirit to indwell them, and a heart to cherish and desire Him. No amount of excellent and knowledgeable and organized parenting will provide a new heart for our child. Therefore, we must *begin* by seeking God and His grace.

This does not eliminate our personal responsibility to do ourselves what is in our power to do. Our main focus in prayer should be seeking from God what He alone can provide. Of course, we are still to pray for the things that we can provide by our own labor, because even those things come from God, as well, through the means of our natural efforts. But we should always do our part, instead of presuming upon God. If I ask God to bless my orange and grapefruit trees in my back yard to yield a good crop of fruit next year, I abuse the practice of calling upon God's Name if I neglect to expend the effort to prune, fertilize, water and spray the trees. Admittedly, God is ultimately the One who makes the tree bear fruit, but He has ordained that

I do what I can do with my natural powers as a part of His work in producing fruit.

Does not this kind of prayer guide find usefulness only for *new* parents, or parents of *small* children? The answer is that all parents, regardless of the ages of their children, need to continue praying the requests on this guide for the long term, ideally as long as they and their children live.

Even (or *especially*) the prayers for salvation should be continued beyond the time of the child's perceived conversion. Do not assume that, since your child has made a profession of faith, and attends Sunday School, and says his prayers at night, that he is therefore *certainly* safe and secure in Jesus and no longer in need of your prayer for his final salvation. Of course, your child may truly have become a Christian at the point of that profession of faith, and if so is certainly saved forever. But we cannot always discern true saving faith, even in our loved ones, until it is tested, and the true believer is the one who perseveres in faith *to the end.*

> Matthew 24:13 "But the one who endures to the end, he shall be saved."

> James 1:12 Blessed is a man who perseveres under trial; for once he has been approved, he will receive the crown of life, which the Lord has promised to those who love Him.

> Hebrews 10:36 For you have need of endurance, so that when you have done the will of God, you may receive what was promised.

Seeing that only those who persevere in faith until the end will be saved, does it not stand to reason that we should continue offering prayer on behalf of our children, that their faith would not fail, and that they would persevere until the end? Even if a child appears to have true faith, he still needs prayer that his faith will continue to live and thrive. Our model should be the encouraging one of Jesus' prayer for His disciple:

> Luke 22:31-32 "Simon, Simon, behold, Satan has demanded permission to sift you like wheat; but I have prayed for you, that your faith may not fail; and you, when once you have turned again, strengthen your brothers."

Parents are therefore encouraged to persevere in prayer for their children, that their faith "may not fail." What this really means is that we must continue to pray that our child will "work out" the salvation that God has "worked in" that child.

> Philippians 2:12-13 So then, my beloved, just as you have always obeyed, not as in my presence only, but now much more in my absence, work out your salvation with fear and trembling; for it is God who is at work in you, both to will and to work for His good pleasure.

One major objective of this prayer guide, therefore, is to help you begin a habit of praying that will last for *many years*, if not *the rest of your life!*

On the next page you can see the whole PRAYER FOR MY CHILD **guide.** At this time, we will introduce the prayer guide and its contents.

Look over the guide before you embark on the explanation section. Familiarize yourself with the order of the requests and the way they are presented. And, you are encouraged to begin using this guide right away for direction in your daily prayer time.

PRAYER FOR MY CHILD

1. Prayer of giving up this child, and presenting him (or her) to the Lord (1 Samuel 1:11, 22, 27; Genesis 22:2, 12, 15-17; Romans 12:1).

2. Prayer for God's blessing on this child (Num. 6:22-27; Matt. 19:13).

3. Prayer for this child's eternal soul, as though today were the last day of his life (Proverbs 27:1).

4. Prayer for this child's spiritual and physical protection (from spiritual and physical harm, kidnapping, abuse, etc.).

5. Prayer for this child's perseverance in faith throughout his life, for God's continued care for his needs should I not survive to see him grown. Prayer for his future marriage partner, etc.

6. Prayer on behalf of this child for grace for his spiritual life in the following areas:

    -Prayer of confession of specific sins which he has committed, prayer for pardon, and for his spiritual healing and restoration. Confession of my own sins as though they were my child's sins. Prayer for my child concerning tendencies in myself and in my spouse that may be passed on to our child (i.e., depression, abuse, slothfulness, etc.).

    -Prayer for grace for my child to love God with all his heart, soul, mind and strength, and his neighbor as himself (Matthew 22:37-40).

    -Prayer for love for God's Word, for his receiving it with glad obedience (especially those commands which specifically address children, such as honoring and obeying parents).

    -Prayer that God would pour out the Spirit of prayer on my child, so that he might develop a habit of prayer early, to continue for his lifetime.

    -Prayer for grace for my child to increasingly desire spiritual pleasures and treasures, as he seeks his happiness in God, and for weaning from love of the treasures and pleasures of this world.

    -Prayer for grace to protect this child against specific temptations which he is now fighting by faith, and the temptations which he can be expected to fight in the future.

    -Prayer for grace for dealing with present and future suffering and trials, and with his fears and sorrows.

    -Prayer for grace for purity and for humility in his life.

    -Prayer for grace for personal ministry and usefulness (use of spiritual gifts, love in relationships, compassion for the lost, opportunities for service and sharing the gospel, school, job, etc.).

    -Prayer for grace to love his enemies, and for a forgiving spirit toward those who persecute or mistreat him (Matthew 5:44; Luke 6:28).

7. Prayer for his physical life and health, and for his material needs.

8. Prayer for specific spiritual needs of this child, from the INVENTORY & EVALUATION sheets.

Dear Stephanie,

    I know that you have a concern that parents might feel overwhelmed when they look at all the items on the guide and evaluation sheets, especially if they have more than one child. How can I explain the way I'm approaching this prayer guide? Some parents, who are devoted, loving parents, and who sincerely desire God's glory and the good of their children, may feel intimidated at first glance. "Is all this necessary when I simply want to pray for my child?" they may ask. How can I help parents see that a prayer guide like this is a needed and beneficial, as well as manageable, approach to this responsibility?

    Remember when we moved back from the West Coast to Florida? While we lived in Seattle, we would fly whenever we went back to the Tampa area to visit our family. From 30,000 feet, we could only see the tops of the clouds and an occasional mountain peak – "peeking" through. On clear days, though you can see forever, you can't see much on the ground.

    But when we moved back to Florida, you remember that I put you and the kids on a plane, and stayed behind in Seattle to load up a Ryder truck. I drove that truck, with all our belongings in it, and towed a trailer with our car on it, all the way across the country. It wasn't until I "got my head out of the clouds," and experienced things at ground level, that I _really_ got a sense of what's between Seattle and Tampa! It's much different braving mountain passes, losing all your radiator water in a desert, almost running out of fuel in the middle of nowhere in Texas, and having to back up on a dead-end street in Louisiana. It's a different ball game when, instead of soaring with the eagles, your loaded-down truck is creeping up the incline of the mountain in Oregon on Interstate 5 at 10 mph, and then playing "runaway truck" down from the mountaintops into northern California!

Though flying certainly appears more efficient, you don't get a feel for the terrain with its endless variations and the vast distances and the slow, steady progress in the seemingly endless striving for your goal. If your _only_ goal is to arrive back east as easily and quickly as possible, then flying seems to be the choice. But the quickest way isn't always best.

Many parents seem to be content to take the fast and easy way. But this book, like the Christian life, is more like traveling on the ground: we are not designed to fly, but must "walk"! We do not want to miss those crucial aspects of our journey, to our and our children's spiritual loss. And, the only way to get to heaven is through slow, methodical, conscientious progress. Of course, sometimes God allows us to "soar with wings as eagles" (Isaiah 40:31). But the daily persevering of the Christian life is more like driving a truck across the mountains and deserts. God has much work to do in us and much to teach us along the way to prepare us for our arrival at our destination!

Love, Tim

Finally, before we are ready to begin the explanation section, please consider the following practical directions.

First, the parent must *adapt this tool to his or her own children and situation.* Simply stated, you must establish a habit of praying for all of these things for each of your children *regularly* and *effectively.* This does *not* mean giving the same amount of time and attention and energy to all of the areas every day. A parent may easily get discouraged if he tries to pray this list exhaustively for each child every day. And, we are not just "going through the motions." The goal is to offer effective, fervent prayer to God to cover our children in all areas of need. To pray *inadequately* every day for *all* the areas will, for all intents and purposes, not be as beneficial as *regular, heartfelt prayer* for *some* areas every day. A *lot* of mediocre, lukewarm, half-hearted prayer will not reach halfway to heaven, but *some* heart-felt, fervent prayer will accomplish much. The parent must ask God for wisdom in determining how often to pray for each area on the list, and when "sufficient" prayer has been offered.

Second, though this prayer list is intended to be fairly comprehensive, you will need to attach additional prayer topics as needed for particular children's needs. Also, a particular child may need more prayer support in one area than another, depending on his personal situation and spiritual needs. Parents are encouraged to use the SPIRITUAL INVENTORY WORKSHEET and the SPIRITUAL PROGRESS EVALUATION WORKSHEET, which are included in PART TWO of this book.

Third, you are encouraged to take the time to read the material according to the way it is presented, and limit your reading to the material allotted for *just one day.* Though many will be tempted to cover the material quickly, and be done with it in less than the prescribed time, there is *great benefit* in taking the time to meditate on it and digest it and master it thoroughly. We are not interested only in gaining knowledge of how to do it, but in reflecting on that knowledge, med-itating on it, making it a part of our thinking, and SEEKING GOD'S GRACE AND POWER. Try to take the sections one by one, and you will receive greater benefit.

Fourth, USE THE **WORD WORKSHEET** AND **SUMMARY PAGE** (located at the end of each week's studies) AS YOU WORK THROUGH EACH DAY'S MATERIAL. These pages are convenient tools to record your thoughts and to identify areas of need.

Fifth, make it a priority to pray for the areas with the *highest importance for eternity*. Think about the aspects of your child's life that will matter a thousand years from now, when this mortal life has long since been buried in the ground. Of course, the temporal concerns should be considered important, too, especially to the extent that they affect eternity.

Sixth, use this prayer approach as a *teaching* tool. *Tell your children what you are doing!* Though the prayer that you offer to the Lord on behalf of your children is largely to be performed in secret, without your child being physically present, he should nevertheless be aware of what you are doing. This is a tremendous teaching tool, as well as means of grace. Not only should your child hear daily your passionate prayers for him during the Family Meeting Time, but he should also know that your pleas for him are not confined to the time of family worship. In addition, explain to your child the meaning of the requests. The explanation that is included in this book is *not only for you*, but to be *passed on to the next generation!* Your child will grow up understanding the *nature and importance and necessity* of prayer in the home on behalf of all the members of that home (including himself), and will see a powerful example of the diligent parent who provides for his child's every need.

Seventh, *pray for God's grace for you and your spouse as praying parents!* Admittedly, we parents desperately need wisdom, love, patience, persistence, consistency, and self-control. These are *graces from God's Spirit*, rather than characteristics that we can produce in ourselves. But we also need to keep in mind that we need God's empowering grace *in order to pray effectively*, as well. Do we sense our total dependence on God for everything in our lives *including the ability to pray?* The Scriptures teach that God pours out the "Spirit of prayer" on us to enable us to pray fervently and effectively.

Zechariah 12:10 "And I will pour out on the house of David and on the inhabitants of Jerusalem, the Spirit of grace and of supplication . . . ."

Romans 8:26 And . . . the Spirit also helps our weakness; for we do not know how to pray as we should, but the Spirit Himself intercedes for us with groanings too deep for words.

The prayer that this book envisions is so much more than merely talking to God. It is dynamic, living, spiritual communion with the personal, though invisible, God. The Holy Spirit must be called upon to enable us to experience that vital communion with God which alone will bring His blessing into our and our children's lives.

PRAYER FOR MY CHILD

EXPLANATION

WEEK 1

Now we begin our explanation of the prayer requests. We will consider the requests one by one, in the order that they appear on the guide.

> **1. Prayer of giving up this child, and presenting him (or her) to the Lord (1 Samuel 1:11, 22, 27; Genesis 22:2, 12, 15-17; Romans 12:1).**

MONDAY

During our first week of learning to pray more effectively and consistently for our children, we will look at the most important and fundamental element of prayer, that of *giving up our children to the Lord.*

The first step in prayer for your child is to "give up" your child to God. Now, at first, this may sound very strange, and almost offensive, to our modern, "evangelical" ears. After all, we tend to think as though God gives us gifts *for our enjoyment in this world,* to enrich our lives *here,* and to "give them up" seems at odds with our common notions about such things. Does God bless us with children, and then require that we give them back to Him?

There is a familiar instance in the Old Testament where Hannah, Samuel's mother, literally gave up her son to the Lord, in fulfillment of an agreement she had made with God. God blessed her with a son, and taking him to the Temple one day, she gave him up to the service of the Lord. The vow that she had made to the Lord is recorded in 1 Samuel:

> 1 Samuel 1:11 And [Hannah] made a vow and said, "O LORD of hosts, if Thou wilt indeed look on the affliction of Thy maidservant and remember me, and not forget Thy maidservant, but wilt give Thy maidservant a son, then I will give him to the LORD all the days of his life, and a razor shall never come on his head."

Though the historical circumstances of this incident are quite unique, and though this passage is not to be understood as teaching that we must literally, physically give up our child to the pastor or the church, the *picture* of giving up the child to the Lord illustrates a crucial aspect of parenting.

Another place where the giving up principle is pictured is in the dramatic narrative of Abraham's "almost-sacrifice" of his son Isaac. This incident, recorded in Genesis 22, has a very important place in the history of redemption. But it is also a powerful picture to parents, since it involves a real-life situation where a father was instructed to *give up his beloved child to the Lord in the most radical way.* Let us consider this astounding passage:

Genesis 22:1-18 Now it came about after these things, that God tested Abraham, and said to him, "Abraham!" And he said, "Here I am." And He said, "Take now your son, your only son, whom you love, Isaac, and go to the land of Moriah; and offer him there as a burnt offering on one of the mountains of which I will tell you."

So Abraham rose early in the morning and saddled his donkey, and took two of his young men with him and Isaac his son; and he split wood for the burnt offering, and arose and went to the place of which God had told him.

On the third day Abraham raised his eyes and saw the place from a distance. And Abraham said to his young men, "Stay here with the donkey, and I and the lad will go yonder; and we will worship and return to you."

And Abraham took the wood of the burnt offering and laid it on Isaac his son, and he took in his hand the fire and the knife. So the two of them walked on together. And Isaac spoke to Abraham his father and said, "My father!" And he said, "Here I am, my son." And he said, "Behold, the fire and the wood, but where is the lamb for the burnt offering?" And Abraham said, "God will provide for Himself the lamb for the burnt offering, my son." So the two of them walked on together. Then they came to the place of which God had told him; and Abraham built the altar there, and arranged the wood, and bound his son Isaac, and laid him on the altar on top of the wood.

And Abraham stretched out his hand, and took the knife to slay his son. But the angel of the LORD called to him from heaven, and said, "Abraham, Abraham!" And he said, "Here I am." And he said, "Do not stretch out your hand against the lad, and do nothing to him; for now I know that you fear God, since you have not withheld your son, your only son, from Me."

Then Abraham raised his eyes and looked, and behold, behind him a ram caught in the thicket by his horns; and Abraham went and took the ram, and offered him up for a burnt offering in the place of his son. And Abraham called the name of that place The LORD Will Provide, as it is said to this day, "In the mount of the LORD it will be provided."

Then the angel of the LORD called to Abraham a second time from heaven, and said, "By Myself I have sworn, declares the LORD, because you have done this thing, and have not withheld your son, your only son, indeed I will greatly bless you, and I will greatly multiply your seed as the stars of the heavens, and as the sand which is on the seashore; and your seed shall possess the gate of their enemies. And in your seed all the nations of the earth shall be blessed, because you have obeyed My voice."

First, we must emphasize that the Holy Spirit's primary intention in this passage is not to teach us about *parenting*, but to teach us about *Christ*. It is meant to focus on Jesus Christ and His all-sufficient sacrifice on the cross as a substitute for our sin. As such, this is a key passage in the Old Testament revelation of God's plan of redemption in His beloved Son.

But the *occasion* for this historical event is *a real-life man's fatherly affection for his precious son*. In this incident Abraham's exclusive love for God is put to the test. Nothing in this world mattered to Abraham more than his son. The test was whether Abraham banked his happiness on the continued enjoyment of his son in this life, or on God. The issue was really whether this doting father was willing to hand over even his only son (through his wife Sarah). The results of the test in the real world proved that Abraham preferred God even to his own beloved son. God was pleased, and stopped Abraham from harming Isaac, saying, "for now I know that you fear God, since you have not withheld your son, your only son, from Me" (Genesis 22:12).

For us as parents, this is a test to see whether we prefer God to our child. Where do we look for satisfaction? We make a god out of whatever we look to for happiness. We can easily deceive ourselves into thinking we really love God Himself, while in reality, we love His gifts. Our children, which are God's *most precious* gifts to us, *can become our gods*. In giving up his only son,

Abraham showed his supreme love for and trust in his heavenly Father, and achieved blessing for himself and his family in Him. Is our relationship with God and our enjoyment of Him the supreme love of our lives, or do we prefer the temporal relations of this world? Or, to put it another way, is our love for our children a love for them *in God and for His sake*, or is it a love for our children *in themselves*? This is a crucial question, because it touches on whether we are really *God*-centered in our affections, or *creature*-centered. We are commanded to *love God with all our heart and mind and soul and strength*. "All" means undivided, exclusive, complete. Ultimately, it is not a matter of loving God *and* loving our children, even if we say we love God more. It is a matter of loving and valuing God *supremely*, to the extent that *everything else* in our lives (including our loved ones) is devoted to the purpose of *advancing in our relationship with Him*. But the wonderful truth is that God desires that we *express* our supreme love for Him precisely in loving these children!

We may say, *"God gave Isaac back to Abraham! He went home with his father!"* Yes! But this happened *only* after Abraham had proved that he had released his emotional hold on his son, and was prepared, for the sake of his relationship with his Lord, to kiss his son good-bye in the most radical way. Abraham could not offer his son to the Lord as a sacrifice, and at the same time *keep* him for his own enjoyment in this world. He had to *entirely give him up*. Fortunately, God does not require all of us to *actually* endure the same kind of test for each of our children! But He *does* require us to *think and live and act and pray as though we are prepared to actually choose life with Him over life with them!* This is how *radical* our giving up of our children is to be.

Obviously God does not want us to literally offer our child as a *burnt* sacrifice, but as a *living* sacrifice (as with our own bodies; Romans 12:1). Of course, the actual, physical sacrifice of our children would be a tremendous affront to God's glory. God makes it clear what He thinks of child sacrifice (see Leviticus 18:21 and 20:2). He does not want us to harm our child, but to *lead our child toward true blessing and happiness*. And, where is real blessing and happiness to be found? Is it found in *our home*, or in *this world's* treasures and pleasures? No, not ultimately. The place where our children are to find true, lasting happiness is not in us and our love, or in this world and its rewards, but in God. So, giving up our children to God is, in the final analysis, the supreme act of love for our children, for only God will bring true joy and happiness.

To give up our children means, first of all, that we look to God alone, and a relationship with Him, as the only happiness for ourselves and for the children we love.

It means also that we really see our children, and pray for them, as *sinners*. Isaac, like every child born with the sin nature of Adam, *deserved* death. In "sacrificing" our child, we are considering fully what we think of his sin. Is his sin obnoxious to us because of its affront to God's glory? Is it the enemy of our child's joy? Then we will be prepared to "put it to death." And, we will see that the only way for our children to be rid of the stain of their sin is to put it to death. Of course, the good news of the Gospel is that, before the supreme punishment for sin is applied to our children (or, to us), *God announces that He has provided a substitute in Christ, and that faith in Him brings life eternal.* But we must *begin* by seeing our children as sinners.

We will begin tomorrow to examine some reasons for asserting that this "giving up" is an essential aspect of parenting, and then explore in what sense we are to "give up" our children to the Lord. ◇

A Note from Stephanie...

Dear Tim,

It seems to me that some are going to read through this section and ask the question, "Are you saying that loving our children isn't okay? 'Cause, if you are, forget it!" (At least that's what *I* would say if *I* misunderstood you!) Obviously, *I* know how much you love our children. You are not suggesting that parents' love for their children be compromised, only more richly endowed with deeper meaning — I wouldn't want you to be misunderstood!

If Melissa were to ask me how my love for her "in Him" is different from the love of a non-believer for her child, what would I say? As you know, I've been thinking a lot about how to put my finger on it. It seems to me that it has to do with what causes my love and delight in her to flourish. Someone else might find their joy in their child's intelligence, looks, special talents, or accomplishments. But *I* get excited when I recognize the ways in which she resembles her Father (not to discount your influence!). Like a widow who sees her son becoming more and more like his father as he grows up, I look for the signs of His likeness in her (and each of

the other children, of course). I delight to see her showing mercy, or being generous or patient or humble. It gives me joy to observe a forgiving spirit or an especially selfless act. In short, I love her "in Him," or "for His sake."

I know that every parent who reads this experiences that love which words cannot express — no matter if the child has special needs or not, is adopted or not, is "just like me" or not — but as Christians, our hearts really sing when the child is "just like Him," don't they?

Love, Stephanie

KEITH–1987

MELISSA–1990

TERESA–1992

CHRISTOPHER–1995

Stephanie,

I certainly don't want to be misunderstood! "If we <u>really</u> love God <u>supremely</u>, are we allowed to love our children?" That's a good question.

I've told you lately that I've grown quite attached to Christopher, as I already had with our other children. You know that, from the very beginning, from the first time I held each one, I have loved him or her more than all the world! Is this allowed? Or, if so, do I love my children <u>too</u> <u>much</u>? I need to know.

Steph, I hope parents understand, as you surely do, that this book is not saying, "Don't love your child," or "Quit loving your children so that you can love God," or "Love God <u>instead</u> of your child." Rather, I am saying, "Love your children <u>in the Lord</u>, and <u>for His sake</u>, and not <u>in themselves</u>." My delight in our children is always <u>also</u> (and <u>mainly!</u>) a delight in their <u>Creator</u>. That makes a world of difference! And that's what's so freeing about distinctively Christian love.

Actually, I find my love for our children is <u>deeper</u> when I love them this way. My experience is that, <u>the more precious God becomes to me, the more precious our children are to me!</u>

Love, Tim

TUESDAY

1. The first reason for giving up our children to God is that they do not belong to us; they belong to another, to God. As Christians, we belong to God. This truth is pictured in the Christian practice of baptism. Baptism means, in part, that a person belongs to God. In baptism, *God's Name* is applied to a person ("in the Name of the Father, and of the Son, and of the Holy Spirit"), which acknowledges that that person belongs to Him. Our children are not given to us to enjoy and to bring up as we please, but to bring up *for God*. They do not belong to us, or to America, or even to themselves, but *to God*. In raising our children, we are preparing them for their *true* Father, and for their *true* Home, in Heaven. As we give them up in prayer to Him every day, we acknowledge that spiritual reality.

Of course, there is a sense in which mankind in general, and so every individual human being, belongs to God. Think of what God says through the prophet Ezekiel:

> Ezekiel 18:4 "Behold, all souls are Mine; the soul of the father as well as the soul of the son is Mine...."

But there is a *special* sense in which people can "belong" to God. He has accomplished redemption in Christ so that He could acquire a people to be His very own possession. God's purpose for redeeming His people is His purpose for our children, as well. His purpose is to redeem and purify a people to be His own precious possession:

> Exodus 19:5 "Now then, if you will indeed obey My voice and keep My covenant, then you shall be My own possession among all the peoples, for all the earth is Mine."

> Titus 2:13-14 ...the blessed hope and the appearing of the glory of our great God and Savior, Christ Jesus; who gave Himself for us, that He might redeem us from every lawless deed and purify for Himself a people for His own possession, zealous for good deeds.

> 1 Corinthians 6:19-20 Or do you not know that...you are not your own? For you have been bought with a price: therefore glorify God in your body.

If our child belongs to God, and if God's purpose in our child's life is to purify him to be His own possession, it seems reasonable for us to regularly acknowledge this fact in some substantial way!

2. The second reason why we must give them up to God is that *He is the One who alone can save and bring my child to true and everlasting happiness.* Our parental priority is to provide for our children's life and happiness. And, we know that the only true and lasting happiness is in the Lord and in fellowship with Him. But that happiness is something that *the Lord Himself* must provide by His grace. No matter how hard we try, no matter how well-versed we are in parenting skills, no matter how good our family seems to be, our efforts cannot save our child. We must hand the child over to the Lord and trust Him to save that child, even as Moses' mother gave him up, putting him in the basket and into the Nile, entrusting him to the providence of God to save him (see Exodus 2:1-10). We are powerless to save our child and to provide him with that which he needs the most for his life and happiness, and must therefore entrust him to God, in Whom alone there is hope for our child.

Without the blessing of the Lord, your best endeavors will do no good. He has the hearts of all men in His hands, and except He touch the hearts of your children by His Spirit, you will weary yourself to no purpose. Water, therefore, the seed you sow on their minds with unceasing prayer.

J. C. Ryle, *"Train Up A Child In The Way He Should Go" (The Duties of Parents)*. (Choteau, MT: Christian Heritage Publisher, 1983), p. 35

In prayer, therefore, we take our child in our arms, and carry him to the Father, and leave him in His care to save him, even as we physically carry our child in our arms to the physician for life-saving treatment. We trust the Great Physician with our child's spiritual well-being, just as we trust our physician with the physical care of the child. Do we trust the Great Physician with such a delicate task, or do we hold back because we somehow think that we could do better than He?

The first act of prayer, therefore, after the diagnosis of our child's hopeless spiritual condition, is to bring him to the Lord, imagining ourselves carrying him in the "arms" of prayer.

3.   The third reason for this prayer concerns us parents and our sanctification. We must daily give them up to God because we can so easily make gods out of our children. This point was made Monday concerning Abraham and his almost-sacrifice of his son Isaac. We tenaciously hold on to our children as our precious possessions, as our delight, as the object of our deepest affection. They *are* precious, and *worth more than all the world!* But God's work in sanctification in our lives is to gradually take away our gods, those objects of our affection that *rival His place in our hearts.* The first commandment is, "You shall have no other gods before Me." The "great and foremost commandment" from Jesus is, "You shall love the Lord your God with *all* your heart, and with *all* your soul, and with *all* your mind" (Matthew 22:37). Yes, our children can *very easily* become our gods! This is seen in how attached we become to them. It is one thing to truly love our children, which is good and proper; it is another thing to bank our earthly happiness in them. It is one thing to passionately seek our children's good; it is quite another thing to passionately *hold on* to them, as though they belong to us, demanding *our right* to them for this life, and therefore blaming God if He takes them away.

If our children have become our gods, what's to say that God *shouldn't* take them away? God's purpose in this life is to take away our idols, one by one, and in the end, He takes them *all* away at our death. But, how perplexed we are when He takes away our idols! How confounded we are when God takes away a beloved relationship, or a cherished possession, that has taken *His* place in our affections. And, how confused and devastated we are when He takes away our children by death from time to time. We ask, *"Why would God do this to me, if He loves me?"* And, we are angry, showing that we believe that we have a right to our children after all, a right that we believe God has unjustly taken away. The problem is that we see our children as God's gift *for our blessing and happiness in this world,* rather than *for His glory and purpose.* We are too "American" in our thinking at this point, and not enough Christian and biblical!

The principle here is, that you must *let go* of your hold on all of your earthly relations, and even your own life, if you are to receive superior and lasting joy in God. If you try to keep your life, you will lose it; if you try to keep your child, you will lose him. True biblical love for the child means that I will give him up for the Lord's sake. This is a requirement of discipleship:

> Matthew 10:37-39 "He who loves father or mother more than Me is not worthy of Me; and he who loves son or daughter more than Me is not worthy of Me. And he who does not take his cross and follow after Me is not worthy of Me. He who has found his life shall lose it, and he who has lost his life for My sake shall find it."

> John 12:25 "He who loves his life loses it; and he who hates his life in this world shall keep it to life eternal."

> Romans 12:1 I urge you therefore, brethren, by the mercies of God, to present your bodies a living and holy sacrifice, acceptable to God, which is your spiritual service of worship.

Certainly the thought of giving our child up can be a troubling one. Does this idea sound scary? It should, if it meant that you were physically releasing your child to the government, or to another human parent, and relinquishing all of your control. But think about it. Why are you praying for your child, anyway? In doing so, you are really giving him up to God. You are bringing the child to the Lord, and leaving the child with Him and asking Him to care for the child according to His will, are you not? The child's life is in God's hands. Actually, in giving up your child to God in your prayer, you are merely acting out what is already true: God does have your child's life in His hands. Who can resist the will of God?

> Ecclesiastes 7:13-14 Consider the work of God, for who is able to straighten what He has bent? In the day of prosperity be happy, but in the day of adversity consider — God has made the one as well as the other so that man may not discover anything that will be after him.

What if it were God's will to take your child by death today? What if your child were to become seriously disabled as the result of an accident or illness? Or, what if one of your children were born with special challenges or needs? This happens to Christians every day. Can you even (in your heart and prayer) hand your child over to *death*, if that is the will of his heavenly Father? Would you be satisfied in God's ways, if He were to do this? Would you trust in His goodness? And, would you be prepared to look to Him, seeking His face and His grace, to sustain you through your time of grief at the staggering loss of your beloved child? Or, would it take you by surprise, sweeping away your peace and joy in believing, because your happiness was tied to your child and not to the Lord? Would you hold back, hanging on to your child and refusing to let him go? The latter may be the case with most professing Christians.

Now is the time to spiritually release your emotional hold on your child, and give him up to the Lord as a *living sacrifice.*   Let this conscious giving up of your child be a picture to you

and to God that the child does not belong to you, and that you have RELEASED him to God, to do with him as He wishes. God is the rightful Parent of your child, and He can be trusted in His wisdom and sovereignty to do what is best for His glory and the good of the child. Entrust the child to the LORD, saying, "I totally trust in Your goodness! Do with this child as You will! Your counter-claim on my child blots out *my* claim on him! I release my claim! I give him up as though he were DEAD, that You may grant him LIFE; otherwise I'll lose him forever." Now is the time to *voluntarily* hand your child over. If he literally died right now, you'd be *forced* to give him up. There's benefit in *freely choosing* to give up this beloved child. Can you do this? Will you do this today? (And, notice that, in the account of Moses' mother in Exodus 2:1-10, it was in "giving him up" that she "got him back," in that she ended up nursing him for Pharaoh's daughter!)

Also: Am I more concerned about the Lord and His will than about my worldly relations? This is a test of that. The Lord must do what glorifies and pleases Him; that is His chief end, His singular passion, His foremost goal. That is also *my* chief end! I must prepare myself, arm myself, with this thinking as I face the *possible* death of my child, and all the anguish that that would bring into my temporal existence. ◇

THURSDAY

One final word on "releasing" as we begin today. I know from many conversations that I've had with believers that this is not our modern way of thinking. Many will rebel against this whole line of reasoning, saying that it may be good theology, but it will not work in the real world. People will tell me that real parents who lose their children are not helped by theology. They might say that the thinking of these pages is too simplistic for sophisticated people in a real world.

But, speaking as a father of four young children, though I have not lost any yet, I think this is the *only* way to approach life and relationships. Of course, it is true that mere theology is not adequate to meet us in life. **But the God of that theology is.** What we are asserting here is that our theology directs us to a God who is sufficient for our needs beyond our wildest imagination (I discovered Him to be so when our Christopher was born with Down Syndrome). Certainly, if I lost any of my children to death, I realize that it would be devastating beyond what I can imagine at this moment.

As I write this, my four children are away on a field trip. They are not safely under my roof, making noise as I work on my computer. If I am realistic, I understand that something may happen to one of my children today out there in that dangerous world. I cannot imagine what it would feel like if that were to happen. But I can say that, if I am looking to God in prayer every day, habitually giving up the child to Him, He can be depended upon to give me grace adequate to even the most devastating experience or loss on earth. My theology tells me that a great God can do more than I can imagine, if I will only look to Him and trust Him.

Tim,

When I think of giving up our children to God, I remember the night before Christopher's surgery. There I was, sitting in bed with his little, twelve-pound body in my arms, snuggled up close and warm as he nursed. As I considered the day that lay ahead, all I could think of was, what if the anesthesiologist made a mistake? or, what if the surgeon sneezed? What if the four and a half months of Christopher's life was to be _all_ of his life? The tears were running down my face as the Lord brought to my mind that most reassuring of verses, "All the days ordained for me were written in your book before one of them came to be" (Psalm 139:16; NIV). He must have been thinking about parents when He gave us that particular truth.

I clung to that assurance that Christopher would live his _whole_ life, just as it had been planned in eternity, whether he would be returned to our arms or not. After all, God loves him even more, and far more perfectly than I do! And He is certainly better able to care for him than I am. The peace that passes understanding was _real_ — and this giving-up prayer is very dear to me.

Love, Stephanie

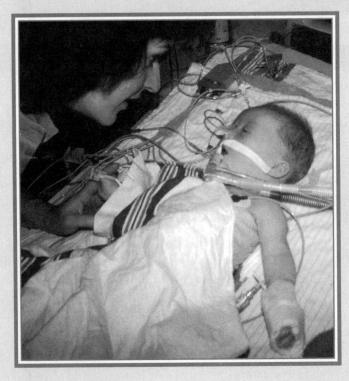

Dear Stephanie,

I know I wrote all this, but I <u>still</u> struggle with this "giving up" thing! Yes, I remember well Christopher's surgery. I couldn't even imagine anything happening to him. How <u>helpless</u> I felt as the orderly pushed his crib-stretcher toward the surgical suite! It almost killed me when I saw Chris' eyes looking at me (he should

have been out cold by then!) as he disappeared through the doors.

Then I ponder the fact that we must <u>spiritually</u> "give them up" like this. Is this realistic? My problem with all of this, I think, is that I think of Christopher as <u>mine</u>, not God's! I have become quite attached to those little people in my home. But is not God free to do as He pleases with Christopher, with what belongs to Him? Or, do I think that I should be free to <u>overrule</u> God in this?

It's when I'm up against the wall in times like these that I really come into touch with what kind of faith I'm living by. Psalm 63:3 says, "Because <u>your love is better than life</u>, my lips will glorify you." (NIV) Do I really live this, no matter what happens to me or to my loved ones? That really is the fight of faith! At helpless times like these, the hardest thing in the world is to affirm Psalm 63:3!

Martin Luther's hymn, "A Mighty Fortress," has these words: "Let goods and kindred go, this mortal life also . . . His Kingdom is forever." Letting the "goods" go, the material things, is manageable . . . maybe. But letting "kindred," loved ones, go (not to mention <u>life itself</u>), well, that's <u>another</u> story! How can anyone do that? "But with God, all things are possible" (Matt. 19:26). Can I say, "Goodbye, little guy," and leave him with God? Pray for me.

Love, Tim

Ephesians 3:20 Now to him who is able to do immeasurably more than all we ask or imagine, according to his power that is at work within us... (NIV)

The challenge here is to always keep this thinking before us and in our prayers.

CONCLUSION: *If I am already truly reconciled in my mind and heart to the fact that my child does not belong to me, but to the Lord, and that his life and well-being are dependent on God, then I will respond differently to what the Lord may do in my child's life. And, if I reconfirm this thinking every day in my prayer, I can trust the Lord to grant me His grace so that, if He does take my child, I will be prepared for that by His grace.*

How does one give up his child to the Lord? By daily consciously acting out, during your prayer time for your child, the offering of him as a living sacrifice to God. Of course, we are not advocating here that we give up our child at the temple in a *physical* sense (or shave his head!), any more than that we give up our physical body literally when we daily offer it as a living sacrifice (Romans 12:1); the child will physically remain in our home.

We must see the passages that we looked at (1 Samuel 1:11 and Genesis 22:1-18), though, as *pictures* of the *attitude* that we should adopt toward God concerning our child.

FRIDAY

OUR RESPONSIBILITY

This "giving up" of the child that we have been considering this week does not mean giving up my responsibility to raise the child. Rather, the contrary is true in this matter. Far from being an *abdication* of responsibility, giving up the child is rather an act of *engaging* ourselves in this responsibility. In talking of "giving up" the child, we are talking about giving up the *possession* of the child, or the *rights* to the child. We are talking about giving up *emotional dependence* on the child, rather than the *responsibility* for the child. We are talking about releasing our claim on that child as a source of happiness or fulfillment or prestige, rather than saying we will have nothing more to do with the child. We give up the child, but at the same time we keep the child for the Lord's sake. Since our children belong to the Lord, we have a *greater* responsibility to be faithful and diligent in caring for them while they are under our care.

Of course, the responsibility to the child involves helping him to finish his journey safely to his true Home, and our setting ourselves apart for God, to be used of Him to protect and guide our child in his pursuit of God. Our responsibility in the bringing up of our children is to show them how precious God is, laboring to recommend Him to them, and keeping Him ever before them as the one and only happiness and joy and treasure and satisfaction forever.

PRAYER FOR MY CHILD

Our responsibility toward God is that we be faithful to Him in the solemn and infinitely important task of bringing up our children toward Him for His glory. The implications of this parental responsibility are brought to light in the following excerpt from a sermon by Jonathan Edwards addressed to a pastor into whose care a church was being committed. Edwards' counsel is directed specifically toward a church's pastor and his responsibility for those entrusted to his care, but God's charge to parents with the care of their children is in many respects exactly the same as His charge to pastors with the care of a flock.

The case with you, *sir*, is as if the head of a family, that was a great prince, with a number of children in a strange land, when going home to receive a kingdom, should leave his children behind him, and commit them to the care of a servant, safely to guide them through a dangerous wilderness, and bring them home to him; in which case, he has their health and lives committed to his care, as well as their future glory in his kingdom. With what care and watchfulness would it be expected of a servant that he should execute his office in such a case? And surely if he fails of being thoroughly careful and watchful, after he has taken upon him so great a charge, and any sad disaster should be the consequence of his unfaithfulness, it will most justly be required of him that he should answer it, and he will inexcusably fall under his master's heaviest displeasure.

And allow me, *sir*, to put you in mind of the account you must give to your master of these souls he seems this day to be about to commit to you: You are to watch for these souls as one that must give account. If any one of these souls should be missing hereafter, having been lost under your ministry, it will be demanded of you another day, by your great Lord, "What is become of such a soul? Here are not all the souls that I committed to you to bring home to me; there is such an one missing; what is become of it? Has it perished through your neglect?" If you are able to say at that time, "Lord, it was not through my neglect; I have done what in me lay for his salvation; I ceased not to warn and counsel and reprove him, and faithfully set before him his danger, and have not forborne to declare thy whole counsel to him; I have not neglected this and other souls that thou didst commit to me, to gratify my laziness, or pursue my worldly interest; I have given myself wholly to this work, laboring therein night and day; I have been ready, Lord, as thou knowest, to sacrifice my own ease and profit, and pleasure, and temporal convenience, and the good will of my neighbors, for the sake of the good of the souls I had the charge of; I have not led this soul into any snare by my ill example; I have neglected no means of thine appointment, either public or private, to turn him from sin to God; I sought out acceptable words, and studied for the most likely means to be used for his saving good; but he would not hearken, but turned a deaf ear; under all [he] was irrational and obstinate, and went on carelessly and disobediently in the imagination of his heart." If you are able to say in like manner as Christ did to the Father, with respect to the souls that were committed to him, *those that thou gavest me I have kept, and none of them is lost, but the son of perdition*, you will be able to hold up your head with comfort before your Judge, your account will be accepted, you shall be acquitted, and your unsuccessful faithfulness shall be rewarded. But if when it shall be demanded of you what is become of such and such souls? you shall be dumb [silent], having nothing to say, your conscience flying in your face, and it shall appear that it has been much the result of your unfaithfulness; O how amazing will your case be! What confusion and astonishment will fill your soul before your great master and Judge! And remember that the blood of such souls will be required at your hands. Ezek. xxxiii. 6.

And allow me, dear brother, to tell you, that you must another day meet these souls that you are now going to take the charge of, before the judgment seat of Christ; and if by means of your faithfulness towards them, in your work, you shall meet them at the right hand of Christ in glory, how joyful a meeting will it be to you! They will be indeed your crown of rejoicing in that day. But if you behold them with devils at the left hand, in horror and despair, your conscience accusing you of unfaithfulness towards them, and it appears that they are lost through your neglect, how amazing will the sight of them be to you!

From the ordination sermon of Rev. Jonathan Judd,
The Great Concern of a Watchman of Souls (1743)

So, as we give up our child to the Lord, at the same time we are affirming our responsibility to raise the child for the Lord. We will someday give an account to Him for how well we fulfilled our responsibility with due diligence and care. In giving our child up to the Lord, we are also giving ourselves up to Him, to serve Him in the responsibility that He has entrusted to us. Ask yourself: Will I be able to give a happy account of my work in the raising of this child? Or, will I hang my head in shame for my failure to discharge my duty?

On that Day on which we will give an account of our faithfulness to the calling to be the parents of our children, much will depend on whether we constantly looked to the Lord in all things, trusting Him with the best interests of our child, and drawing on His grace for the fulfillment of our responsibility. ◇

SATURDAY

Today, as we close our week-long consideration of the daily discipline of "giving up" our child to the Lord, we will review the main points of our material, meditate upon the teaching, and offer to God a special prayer for His enabling grace as we embark on the very serious and solemn task of praying for our children.

As we saw, the picture of Samuel's mother, Hannah, giving up her child to the Lord illustrates a crucial aspect of parenting.

1 Samuel 1:11 And [Hannah] made a vow and said, "O LORD of hosts, if Thou wilt indeed look on the affliction of Thy maidservant and remember me, and not forget Thy maidservant, but wilt give Thy maidservant a son, then I will give him to the LORD all the days of his life, and a razor shall never come on his head."

What are the reasons that we discovered for "giving up" our children to the Lord? Let us review them once more and set aside some serious time to conscientiously meditate upon them, pray about them, and consider their implications for our prayer life for our children and for our approach to parenting in general:

1. The first reason for giving up our children to God is that they do not belong to us; they belong to another, to God.

Ezekiel 18:4 "Behold, all souls are Mine; the soul of the father as well as the soul of the son is Mine...."

Exodus 19:5 "Now then, if you will indeed obey My voice and keep My covenant, then you shall be My own possession among all the peoples, for all the earth is Mine."

Titus 2:13-14 ...the blessed hope and the appearing of the glory of our great God and Savior, Christ Jesus; who gave Himself for us, that He might redeem us from every lawless deed and purify for Himself a people for His own possession, zealous for good deeds.

1 Corinthians 6:19-20   Or do you not know that...you are not your own? For you have been bought with a price: therefore glorify God in your body.

2.   The second reason why we must give them up to God is that *He is the One who alone can save and bring my children to true and everlasting happiness.*

Psalm 127:1 Unless the LORD builds the house, they labor in vain who build it.

Without the blessing of the Lord, your best endeavors will do no good. He has the hearts of all men in His hands, and except He touch the hearts of your children by His Spirit, you will weary yourself to no purpose. Water, therefore, the seed you sow on their minds with unceasing prayer.
J. C. Ryle, *"Train Up A Child In The Way He Should Go" (The Duties of Parents)*, p. 35

3.   The third reason concerns *us parents and our sanctification.* **We must daily give them up to God because we can so easily make** *gods* **out of our children.**

Matthew 10:37-39 "He who loves father or mother more than Me is not worthy of Me; and he who loves son or daughter more than Me is not worthy of Me. And he who does not take his cross and follow after Me is not worthy of Me. He who has found his life shall lose it, and he who has lost his life for My sake shall find it."

John 12:25 "He who loves his life loses it; and he who hates his life in this world shall keep it to life eternal."

Romans 12:1 I urge you therefore, brethren, by the mercies of God, to present your bodies a living and holy sacrifice, acceptable to God, which is your spiritual service of worship.

ITEMS FOR PRAYER

As we close out this week of foundational concerns in our life of prayer for our children, we have no doubt sensed the seriousness and immenseness of our task as parents. As we said at the beginning of our study, ***prayer is the place to start in child rearing***. We could say that this statement has more than one application. When it was stated at the beginning, it referred to the crucial importance of our diligent prayer for the good of our children. But also, we must say that prayer is the place to start when we consider the vast and sober responsibilities that have been entrusted to us as parents. How dependent we are on the Lord through the means of prayer!

We also must realize that we *cannot even pray* as we should without the grace and help of the Spirit (see Romans 8:26). Who can pray for such things in the power of the flesh?

So, let us enter a pattern of serious prayer as a result of our time this week considering these things. ***For what shall we pray specifically?***

Pray for God's special enabling for you to receive whatever He does in your life and in the life of your child. Pray not only that you would accept it, but that you would be prepared and strengthened in your heart to embrace whatever happens as in God's control and part of His good and wise plan for your good and His glory. Pray that you would be satisfied in God's ways, trusting in His goodness.

Pray that God would enable you to release your emotional hold on your child, and give him up to the Lord as a living sacrifice. Entrust the child to the LORD, saying, "I totally trust in Your goodness! Do with this child as You will! Your counter-claim on my child blots out my claim on him! I release my claim! I give him up as though he were DEAD, that You may grant him LIFE; otherwise I'll lose him forever."
     Establish the daily discipline of looking to God in prayer, habitually giving up your child to Him, knowing that He can be depended upon to give you grace adequate to cover even the most devastating experience or loss on earth. *"Now to him who is able to do immeasurably more than all we ask or imagine, according to his power that is at work within us..."* (Ephesians 3:20; NIV)

Pray that you would be truly reconciled in your mind and heart to the fact that your child does not belong to you, but to the Lord. Pray that you would be reconciled to the fact that his life and well-being are dependent on God. Reconfirm this thinking every day in your prayer, so that, if God does take your child, you would be prepared for that by His grace.

Pray for God's grace in your responsibility of raising the child for Him. Far from being an abdication of responsibility, giving up the child is rather an act of engaging ourselves in this responsibility. In talking of "giving up" the child, we are talking about giving up the possession of the child, the rights to the child, and the emotional dependence on the child, rather than the responsibility for the child.

A copy of these prayer requests is included at the conclusion of this study for your convenience. You are also encouraged to go back and read the quote from Jonathan Edwards about a pastor's responsibility for those under his care (page 33), and freshly apply it to your own responsibility as a parent. Use it as a guide for your reflection and prayer.
     𝔓arental 𝔠ovenant to 𝔓ray 𝔉or 𝔐y 𝔠hildren. Use the Covenant on the next page to commit yourself to the discipline of prayer for your children (Sunday would be an appropriate time to sign this Covenant). It will then be a reminder in the days ahead of a solemn agreement that you have made with God to be faithful in your responsibility. Also, though, it will serve as a witness against you if you fall back on your responsibility. Keep in mind that, unless you are prepared to sign such a Covenant, vowing before the Lord to be faithful in your part on behalf of your children, all of the material in these pages will not likely do you or your children much good. In your willingness to *commit yourself* to such an endeavor as prayer for your child, you show that your heart is truly in it. God will bless your wholehearted devotion. ◇

[NOTE: A duplicate copy of this Covenant is provided at the conclusion of this study series.
You may sign both copies, and post the duplicate in a conspicuous place as a daily reminder.]

Parental Covenant to Pray For My Children

I hereby release each child to my Lord, affirming to Him:

"I totally trust in Your goodness. Do with this child as You will. Your counter-claim on my child erases my claim on him. I release my claim. I give him up as though he were dead, that You may give him new life that will last forever. I am reconciled in my heart and mind to the fact that my child does not belong to me, but to You, whose love is greater than my own, and that his life and well-being are totally dependent on You. I will look to You daily to bless my child and save him and keep him in Your care. And, as I daily reconfirm this thinking in my prayer, I can trust You so that, if You do take my child from me, I will be prepared by Your grace."

I hereby confirm my responsibility for each child my Lord has entrusted to my care. By His grace, I resolve to not be negligent in my responsibility for each child:

"I give myself wholly to do whatever I can for his salvation night and day, sacrificing worldly interests and profit for his eternal good. I will not cease to faithfully set before him his danger, and will declare Your whole Word to him. I will not lead this soul into any snare by my ill example. I will not neglect any means that You have appointed to turn him from sin to God. I especially now solemnly commit myself to pray faithfully for my child daily, as I am guided by this prayer list and explanation."

Name(s) of child(ren):_____

_____

Parental Signature:_____ Date:_____

Witnesses:_____

Stephanie,

How do I feel about this Covenant? At first, I'm not sure I feel comfortable about signing this. After all, you sign things in the secular world that commit you to temporal things, like paying back a loan. I know that signing a covenant, with witnesses, is a pretty serious thing! I know what it means if I sign a legal contract and then fail to fulfill what it says. The more that is at stake, the more important the signing.

This covenant is like the Christian life. In taking a vow, I acknowledge that God will judge me if I do not fulfill my vow. Of course, God will hold you to His terms whether you take a covenant seriously or not! As I write this, a hurricane is headed toward Florida. And, this hurricane, if it hits, is coming whether I welcome it or not. So it is with God's judgment.

It's so easy to be distracted by the cares and pleasures of this life. Or, it is so easy, when we find the road difficult, to turn back. How prone we are to give up and no longer give ourselves to a demanding responsibility to which we have committed ourselves. I need to be constantly reminded of the agreement that I have made with the Lord.

The success of this prayer endeavor, from the human perspective, depends on our _perseverence_ in that prayer. Of course, prayer is founded on the understanding that we are not in control. Success is not because we are using the best prayer guide on the planet, or because we really work hard at it, but because of God's grace. But if we are dependent on God for _physical_ life, that doesn't mean there's no point in _breathing_! It's the same with prayer. We must do our part.

The Covenant is signed because of the nature of prayer as a life-long commitment. You don't just do it and then you're finished. George Mueller, the famous 19th Century Christian, wrote that he had prayed for requests for 19 years and 6 months, without missing a single day! That's the extent of most children's time at home! Can we say we've prayed like that? We don't all have the kind of resolve that Mueller had. But, as we sign this covenant together, let us resolve, by God's grace, to engage ourselves in earnest to pray daily for our children!

Love, Tim

A Note from Stephanie...

Tim,

I do love the Parental Covenant to Pray for my Children. The first statement is exactly what I want to say to the Lord on behalf of each one of our precious children. I hope to have it virtually memorized soon. I feel that I am placing the hand of each child into His hand each day — just where I want it.

The second statement confirming my responsibility is very awesome, to the point of taking my breath away as I consider it. But I do embrace it, because it is the deepest desire of my heart to be committed to every aspect of it. How much I need to memorize it, as time goes by, so that it may be a lighthouse to me in the storms and quiets of every day.

It is encouraging to me in my personal weakness to remember that, as you have said many times, God is requiring of me as a parent that I <u>look to Him by faith in His wonderful grace</u>. I know that I will not keep this covenant <u>perfectly</u>, but the important thing is that I continually depend upon His grace to enable me to be faithful to the task before me. I have not the strength in myself to do it. I see that I cannot pray for my children without praying for their mother, too!

Love, Stephanie

Personal Meeting Time:

THE WORD

The Word Preached / Taught

Scripture Reading

Personal Reading / Study

SUNDAY

Sermon / teaching:

Scripture reading:

Personal reading / study:

Items for Prayer

MONDAY

Scripture reading: 1 Samuel 1:1-28; Genesis 22:1-18; Romans 12:1

Personal reading / study:

Items for Prayer

TUESDAY

Scripture reading: Ezekiel 18:4; Exodus 19:5; Titus 2:13-14;
1 Corinthians 6:19-20; Exodus 2:1-10; Psalm 127:1

Personal reading / study:

Items for Prayer

WEDNESDAY

Scripture reading: Matthew 22:37; Matthew 10:37-39; John 12:25; Romans 12:1; Ecclesiastes 7:13-14

Personal reading / study:

Items for Prayer

THURSDAY

Scripture reading: Ephesians 3:20; Romans 12:1; 1 Samuel 1:11

Personal reading / study:

Items for Prayer

FRIDAY

Scripture reading: Ezekiel 33:1-9; review the passages already meditated upon this week, and reflect on the quote on page 33

Personal reading / study:

Items for Prayer

SATURDAY

Scripture reading: Ez 18:4; Ex 19:5; Titus 2:13-14; 1 Cor 6:19-20; Psalm 127:1; Matt 10:37-39; John 12:25; Rom 12:1; Eccl 7:13-14

Personal reading / study:

Items for Prayer

WEEK 1 – SUMMARY SHEET
Guiding Questions

[**NOTE:** *These questions, which are to be answered in the spaces below, are to guide you in reflecting on each day's content.* **All** *of the questions will not be answered* **every** *day, but only those that are helpful in processing a particular day's material.*]

1. In what specific ways has my thinking and practice been challenged or transformed by my interaction with today's biblical teaching? What particular teaching will require further study and reflection?

2. For what specific wrong thinking, sinful priorities, or areas of neglect in my responsibility, must I make confession and seek the forgiveness of the Lord?

3. Seeing that I am now responsible to strive to make the Word I have received today a reality in my life, what specifically must I do in response to God? How specifically will my life and relationships be different as a result of my time with God today? What vows might I make to the Lord this Sunday regarding my intentions to be faithful to Him in particular areas? And, seeing that, in order for this life change to become a reality, God must powerfully work by His grace and through His Spirit in my life, what specifically must I ask God to do or provide?

4. Upon what particular Bible verses will I meditate throughout the day? What verses do I desire to post in a conspicuous place to remind me to meditate upon them? What verses will I commit to memory?

MONDAY

TUESDAY

WEDNESDAY

THURSDAY

FRIDAY

SATURDAY

PRAYER FOR MY CHILD

EXPLANATION

WEEK 2

We begin now our second week in considering the guide. We have spent a week on the first prayer request because of the foundational nature of that request to all that we pray for on behalf of our children. This week we will spend our time considering specific prayer for our children's salvation.

MONDAY

> **2. Prayer for God's blessing on this child (Numbers 6:22-27; Matthew 19:13).**

I have already given my child up to the Lord. Now what? Today we will consider the second request, for God's blessing to rest on our child. Not only am I giving the child up to the Lord, but I am pleading with God that His blessing will rest on my child as a consequence of my action. What is my supreme concern for my child? What do I want for him more than anything else? Is it that he would experience the joy of seeing and prizing and delighting in the glory of the Lord forever? This is what the blessing is all about, and this is what we are praying for in the second petition for our child.

This principle is illustrated by the biblical picture of baptism. In baptizing a person, we are acting out what we call upon the Lord to do, that He would bless the person. We are not actually *doing* what this picture points to, but are *calling upon God to apply the blessing* to which the picture points. To "call God's Name" upon a person means to ask God to bless that person. Meditate for a few minutes on this, the ultimate passage on blessing in the Bible:

> Numbers 6:22-27 Then the LORD spoke to Moses, saying, "Speak to Aaron and to his sons,
>   saying, 'Thus you shall bless the sons of Israel. You shall say to them:
> The LORD bless you, and keep you;
>   The LORD make His face shine on you, and be gracious to you;
> The LORD lift up His countenance on you, and give you peace.'
>   So they shall invoke My name on the sons of Israel, and I then will bless them."

What is blessing? Sometimes we think of blessing mainly in terms of the things of this world and this life. In the Bible, however, blessing points to beholding the glory of God, to having the beauty and radiance and excellence of the divine glory shine upon us. To be blessed is to dwell in the presence of God, beholding His face, forever. This is what Numbers 6 teaches. And, as it says in that passage, receiving the blessing is pictured in the Bible by having His Name placed upon us.

Salvation means that God writes His Name on your head, your hand, and your heart.
                                                                          -Edmund Clowney

Many parents err at this point, and expose their children to eternal ruin. The mistake is often made in assuming that a child is automatically, by creation, God's child. Or, at least, they assume that a child is too young to be in danger of something that he is unable to understand or do anything about (we will look at this later in this series of studies). While there is a sense in which all human beings are God's "children" by creation (see Acts 17:28-29), that does not mean that they are born safe and secure from harm because they are "innocent" and God is their "Father." The Scriptures teach that people in this fallen world are born into Satan's family, not God's.

Psalm 51:5 Behold, I was brought forth in iniquity, and in sin my mother conceived me.

Romans 3:23 For all have sinned and fall short of the glory of God.

1 John 3:12 Do not be like Cain, who belonged to the evil one and murdered his brother. And why did he murder him? Because his own actions were evil and his brother's were righteous. (NIV)

John 8:42-43 Jesus said to them, "If God were your Father, you would love Me; for I proceeded forth and have come from God, for I have not even come on My own initiative, but He sent Me. Why do you not understand what I am saying? It is because you cannot hear My word. You are of your father the devil, and you want to do the desires of your father. He was a murderer from the beginning, and does not stand in the truth, because there is no truth in him. Whenever he speaks a lie, he speaks from his own nature; for he is a liar, and the father of lies."

1 John 3:8 The one who practices sin is of the devil; for the devil has sinned from the beginning. The Son of God appeared for this purpose, that He might destroy the works of the devil.

1 John 3:10 By this the children of God and the children of the devil are obvious: anyone who does not practice righteousness is not of God, nor the one who does not love his brother.

Since our children are sinners by birth and practice sin as soon as they are able, and therefore are born into Satan's "family," their only hope is to be "adopted" into God's Family through His Son. This truth is pictured by the saints in Old Testament times in physically leaving their families to go with the Lord where He would take them:

Genesis 12:1 Now the LORD said to Abram, "Go forth from your country, and from your relatives and from your father's house, to the land which I will show you."

Joshua 24:2 And Joshua said to all the people, "Thus says the LORD, the God of Israel, 'From ancient times your fathers lived beyond the River, namely, Terah, the father of Abraham and the father of Nahor, and they served other gods. Then I took your father Abraham from beyond the River, and led him through all the land of Canaan, and multiplied his descendants and gave him Isaac."

The picture of *adoption* in the New Testament points to our being adopted into God's Family, and receiving a "new Name," and is a very powerful picture of what God does in our salvation.

Romans 8:15   For you have not received a spirit of slavery leading to fear again, but you have received a spirit of adoption as sons by which we cry out, "Abba! Father!"

Galatians 4:4-5   But when the fulness of the time came, God sent forth His Son, born of a woman, born under the Law, in order that He might redeem those who were under the Law, that we might receive the adoption as sons.

Ephesians 1:5   He predestined us to adoption as sons through Jesus Christ to Himself, according to the kind intention of His will.

In praying daily that our child will receive God's blessing, we are praying that God would do in the life of our child what baptism points to. We know that the child must "receive a new Name," God's Name, and be called "Christian," in order to receive the blessing. He must leave Satan's family and be joined to God's Family through union with Christ.

So, let us pray during this time every day that God would bless our child, that He would place His Name on him, and that our child will dwell happily in God's presence forever.

Matthew 19:13-15   Then some children were brought to Him so that He might lay His hands on them and pray; and the disciples rebuked them. But Jesus said, "Let the children alone, and do not hinder them from coming to Me; for the kingdom of heaven belongs to such as these." And after laying His hands on them, He departed from there.

TUESDAY

> ### 3. Prayer for this child's eternal soul, as though today were the last day of his life (Proverbs 27:1).

Now we will touch on a most essential prayer focus. In a way, it is praying for the same thing for which we have been praying in the first two requests that we have considered. We have given our child over to the Lord, and have asked for His divine blessing to reside on that child. Today, we take those two requests one step further, asking specifically that God would save this child from his sin and the hell that he deserves, and deliver this child into salvation.

Obviously the priority in praying for our child is his eternal well-being. This priority will ring loud and clear as we consider several quotes from wise teachers in the church of the past. Take the time to read through these quotes very carefully.

We must make prayer for our children's salvation our #1 PRIORITY. Very often parents are so concerned about their children's temporal, worldly well-being that relatively little attention is given to the discipline of prayer on behalf of the children. We diligently and with great commitment train our children to be successful in this world, but very little purposeful effort, it seems, is given to an infinitely more important matter, training for eternity. Think of the sobering words of J. C. Ryle:

...no part of [your children] should be so dear to you as that part which will never die. The world, with all its glory, shall pass away; the hills shall melt; the heavens shall be wrapped together as a scroll; the sun shall cease to shine. But the spirit which dwells in those little creatures, whom you love so well, shall outlive them all, and whether in happiness or misery (to speak as a man) will depend on you.

This is the thought that should be uppermost on your mind in all you do for your children. In every step you take about them, in every plan, and scheme, and arrangement that concerns them, do not leave out that mighty question, *'How will this affect their souls?'*

Soul love is the soul of all love. To pet and pamper and indulge your child, as if this world was all he had to look to, and this life the only season for happiness — to do this is not true love, but cruelty....It is hiding from him that grand truth, which he ought to be made to learn from his very infancy, — that the chief end of his life is the salvation of his soul.

A true Christian must be no slave to fashion, if he would train his child for heaven. He must not be content to do things merely because they are the custom of the world; to teach them and instruct them in certain ways, merely because it is usual; to allow them to read books of a questionable sort, merely because everybody else reads them; to let them form habits of a doubtful tendency, merely because they are the habits of the day. He must train with an eye to his children's souls. He must not be ashamed to hear his training called singular and strange. What if it is? The time is short, — the fashion of this world passeth away. He that has trained his children for heaven, rather than for earth, — for God, rather than for man, — he is the parent that will be called wise at last.

J. C. Ryle, *"Train Up A Child In The Way He Should Go" (The Duties of Parents)*, pp.8-9

1. We must pray FERVENTLY and PASSIONATELY for the salvation of our children. It is helpful in this aspect of our duty to think about the powerful picture of a woman in labor at the birth of her child. In a sermon entitled, "Travailing for Souls," on Isaiah 66:8, preached Sunday, September 3, 1871, Charles Spurgeon said the following:

Do any of you desire your children's conversions? You shall have them saved when you agonize for them. Many a parent who has been privileged to see his son walking in the truth will tell you that before the blessing came, he had spent many hours in prayer and in earnest pleading with God, and then it was that the Lord visited his child and renewed his soul....Why is it that there must be this anxiety before desirable results are gained? For answer, it might suffice us to say that God has so appointed it. It is the order of nature. The child is not born into the world without the sorrows of the mother, nor is the bread which sustains life procured from the earth without toil: 'In the sweat of thy face shalt thou eat bread,' was part of the primeval curse. Now, as it is in the natural, so is it in the spiritual; there shall not come the blessing we seek, without first of all the earnest yearning for it. Why, it is so even in ordinary business. We say, 'No sweat no sweet,' 'No pains no gains,' 'No mill no meal.' If there be no labor there shall be no profit. He that would be rich must toil for it: he that would acquire fame must spend and be spent to win it. It is ever so. There must ever be the travail and then the desire cometh. God has so appointed it: let us accept the decree.

Charles Spurgeon, *Spurgeon's Expository Encyclopedia* (Baker), vol. 13, pp. 258-59

The powerful picture of a mother in labor in the birth of a child should govern our thinking and acting regarding our prayer for our children. God Himself points to the picture of childbirth when He speaks of the entrance of the newly converted person into the spiritual life. The apostle Paul uses the picture of being in labor in childbirth to describe his fervent longing on behalf of the Galatians:

Galatians 4:19 My children, with whom I am again in labor until Christ is formed in you....

Think of the experience of giving birth to a child, and then apply that picture to prayer for the *rebirth* of our children. Just as the labor pains preceded the physical birth of our child when God brought this child forth, so also we will be "in labor" in prayer for his *new* birth.

Do we think this way? Do we reflect on that day (or night!) when our child was born? Do we think of the passions and pain and preoccupation that we had concerning that long hoped-for birth? And, do we apply that to the child's *spiritual* birth? (See Lamentations 2:19!) ◇

A Note from Stephanie...

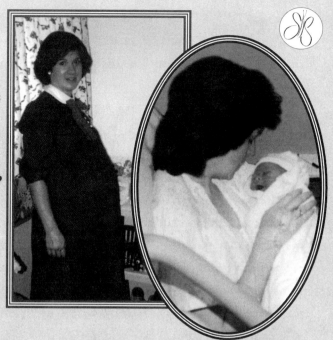

Tim,

Oh, childbirth! Oh, labor! Oh, dear! What an experience to compare our prayers for salvation to! Remember the first time, how I struggled against it? And the second, when it seemed that there would never be any progress? I was so grateful for the assistance that was offered when I needed it. (That's what I think of when I look at the Prayer Guide — it's assistance to make more effective progress!)

I was glad that #3 and #4 were quicker, but I was especially happy to have had additional instruction in how to work _with_ the labor, rather than trying to mentally remove myself from it — being engaged, rather than struggling for detachment. That's how I want to labor in love in prayer for Keith, Melissa, Teresa, and Christopher — as informed, aware, and purposefully in pursuit of the goal as I can be!

I feel the need to note that many parents have already experienced the joy of observing the spiritual birth of their children. Such a father or mother might read through all this encouragement regarding prayer for salvation as not applicable to them, but because I love many such brothers and sisters in the Lord, I want to emphasize one key thing that you mention. The ones who are saved are the ones who _persevere_. Who among us does not know the sad tale of a youngster, full of spiritual zeal, who became caught in the world's snares, and ended up in misery, apart from the Lord? Though youthful professions, like that of Timothy in the Scripture, are often borne out over a lifetime, parents must diligently persevere in prayer for the growth and strengthening of that precious bud of faith. The gardener must not relax when the bud appears, but must labor on for the blooms and fruit to be produced. May we, too, be constant and vigilant in our care of the souls entrusted to us, to God's glory!

Love, Stephanie

Stephanie,

I'm sure you remember that I was there for the births of all our children. I went through a lot! Remember how you felt so sorry for me? I was a mess!

In all seriousness, it was heart-wrenching for me to see you go through what you went through, and I felt so helpless to provide relief. I remember so vividly those seemingly endless labors for Keith and Melissa. Teresa was born twenty minutes after our arrival at the hospital, and I was so relieved that she came so quickly! Christopher was the quickest yet, but still was no picnic. Whew! Remember Kathy, the woman in our church who, when I visited after she gave birth, commented about how upset she was with _Eve_? She really messed things up for women when she ate that apple! What an experience labor is.

What a joy, though, when the child was born! I was the first to see Melissa's face when she emerged into a bright, cold world. Her face was expressionless at first, as if sound asleep. Then all of a sudden, as the air hit her face, she _gasped_ - she looked as if someone had thrown a glassful of Puget Sound ice water into her face (we were living in Seattle). Then she cried her little head off. I'll never forget that face!

What a thrill it is to hold a new life in my hands. (I have been tempted to say, "Now that I see the baby, it was _worth_ all that pain!" but I wouldn't dare . . .) But it didn't come easy, did it?

New birth doesn't come easy, either! Of course, the pain that was necessary to our _rebirth_ was borne by Christ on the cross, but we parents must do our part. And labor is a powerful picture of parental prayers.

Unless we let those terrible contractions do their work, we can't expect that the "baby" will get born. There must be labor before birth . . . and, we may think it is going to be easier than it turns out to be.

Now that I grasp this truth, I have attempted praying "labor prayers." Our goal in this second round of labor pangs is the _rebirth_ of all our children! But, Steph, how feeble my attempts are toward our children's rebirth in comparison to your labor for these same children's physical births! Romans 8:26 is encouraging, when it says that the Spirit helps us in our weakness when we pray, producing groanings too deep for words. Here's to more successful experiences in labor together!

Love, Tim

2. We must pray DILIGENTLY and TIRELESSLY.

Spurgeon also said the following, in another sermon:

WEDNESDAY

> I must not speak for you; but I may speak for myself. If there be anything I know, anything that I am quite assured of beyond all question, it is that praying breath is never spent in vain. If no other man here can say it, I dare to say it, and I know I can prove it. My own conversion is a result of prayer, long, affectionate, earnest, and importunate. Parents prayed for me; God heard their cries, and here I am to preach the Gospel. Since then I have ventured upon some things that were far beyond my capacity as I thought; but I have never failed because I have cast myself upon the Lord.

The following account is of the attitude of Sarah Edwards, the wife of Jonathan Edwards:

> She thought that, as a parent, she had great and important duties to do towards her children, before they were capable of government and instruction. For them, she constantly and earnestly prayed, and bore them on her heart before God, in all her secret and most solemn addresses to him; and that, even before they were born. The prospect of her becoming the mother of a rational immortal creature, which came into existence in an undone and infinitely dreadful state, was sufficient to lead her to bow before God daily, for his blessing on it — even redemption and eternal life by Jesus Christ. So that, through all the pain, labor, and sorrow, she was in travail for them, that they might be born of God.
> Jonathan Edwards, *Works*, vol. One (Edinburgh: Banner of Truth, 1974, orig. 1834), p. xlv.

Consider this testimony to Jonathan Edwards' parents' prayers for him:

> Many were the prayers presented by parental affection that this only and beloved son might be filled with the Holy Spirit; from a child know the Holy Scriptures; and be great in the sight of the Lord. They who thus fervently and constantly commended him to God, manifested equal diligence in training him up for God. Prayer excited to exertion, and exertion again was encouraged by prayer.
> Jonathan Edwards, *Works*, vol. One, p. xii

Let the fervency and diligence of the prayers of these people for the conversion of their children be a powerful example to us all. Very few Christians today, it seems, would be eligible for the criticism that they pray too much and too passionately for their children's *eternal* well-being! How many parents today make their children's everlasting joy their utmost concern? How many give attention to eternal pursuits, spiritual treasures in God, in proportion to their importance and worth? More often, almost all attention and devotion are given to the earthly, material pursuits of our children to the neglect of what is really important.

And, even among Christian parents who are devoted to their children's spiritual advancement, there is often neglect of the most important aspect of the development of the child's spiritual life, that being prayer for him. Be shocked by this tragic story related by Richard Pratt:

> I once spoke with an older woman reputed to be a prayer warrior. Church members frequently asked her to pray for their special needs. When I questioned this woman about her devotion to prayer, she told me this story with tears in her eyes. Early in her adult life she was widowed and left with a son.

She devoted herself to making this son the finest Christian man possible. She read books on rearing children; she sent him to the best schools; she spent great quantities of time with him. "But," she confessed, "I hardly ever prayed for him." Her story had a tragic ending. Beset with one failure after another, her twenty-five-year-old son committed suicide. "Only then," she said, "did I see that I had depended too much on myself and not enough on God." So today she devotes herself to prayer. She turns from creaturely impotence to the omnipotent Creator. Tragic experiences like this demonstrate the importance of relying on God and not on our own feeble strength. He is our Sovereign; our destinies lie in His hands. For this reason, looking to God in prayer is an essential part of the Christian life.

Richard L. Pratt, Jr., *Pray With Your Eyes Open*
(Phillipsburg, New Jersey: Presbyterian and Reformed Publishing Company, 1987), p. 18.

THURSDAY

3. **Pray for your children's conversion as you would pray for anyone's conversion.** The following is a summary of the kinds of prayers used in Scripture for people's conversion. These are the kind of prayers that we should offer for our children's salvation:

> *"God, remove from him (or her) that heart of stone and give him a heart of flesh."* (Ezekiel 11:19)
> *"Lord, circumcise his heart, so that he may love you with all his heart and with all his soul, and live."* (Deuteronomy 30:6)
> *"God, make him, who is dead in transgressions and sin, alive in Christ by Your Spirit."* (Ephesians 2:1-5)
> *"Father, let Your light shine in his heart, to give him the light of the knowledge of the glory of God in the face of Christ."* (2 Corinthians 4:6)
> *"Lord, save him through the washing of rebirth and renewal by the Holy Spirit."* (Titus 3:5)
> *"Father, grant him repentance leading him to a knowledge of the truth, that he will come to his senses and escape from the trap of the devil."* (2 Timothy 2:25, 26)
> *"Lord, open his heart to believe and respond to the Gospel."* (Acts 16:14)
> *"Father, put your Spirit in him and move him to follow Your decrees and be careful to keep Your laws."* (Ezekiel 36:27)

4. **Pray as though it were the last day of your child's life, and as though you will never again have another chance to pray for him.** We thought of our child's possible death in our consideration of the first prayer for our child. In our age of advanced medicine, childhood death is not nearly as prevalent as it used to be. My sister died in 1952, when she was eight years old, of a disease (polio) that is not a threat to our children today, thanks to medical advances. But children still die every day of cancer or other diseases. Every one of us knows a family, perhaps our own family, that has suffered the tragic loss of a child to death. Of course, many children die in accidents, as well. *I challenge you to really take this seriously.* Your child may die. Imagine your child's picture at the front of the church during his memorial service. Would that dread thought motivate you to pray for him? Get in touch with your child's MORTALITY. *(Continued on page 53)*

Dear Stephanie,

As you know, this little girl is my sister, Deanie. Those who knew her remember her as an especially sweet child. The family was moving back to the East Coast after living in California while Dad served in the Marine Corps during the Korean War. During the car trip across the country, Deanie suddenly fell ill, and died within hours at a hospital in a little town in Wyoming. She was only 8 years old. My mother has shared with me about Deanie's last days on earth. It still tears your heart out.

I was born a little over a year after she died, and was brought up under the shadow of her death, and my parents' grief. Her little grave is about five minute's drive from my house. I went over today, and stood there and pondered her life. And I thought about my own children.

Death is the _last_ thing I think about when I look at our children! I simply can't bear the thought of one of our children dying. How could one ever adequately prepare for the death of a child? But the sad truth is, children die.

Steph, do we think of our children as mortal? Do we ponder the possibility of their death? Do we pray as though this day were their last?

Love, Tim

DIANA MARIE
SPILMAN
MAR. 16, 1944
JUNE 9, 1952

LORD KEEP US SAFE THIS NIGHT,
SECURE FROM ALL OUR FEARS.
MAY ANGELS WATCH US
WHILE WE SLEEP
TIL MORNING LIGHT APPEARS

A Note from Stephanie...

Dear Tim,

Our ability to contemplate mortality is certainly one that grows as we mature, isn't it? As a child in the first grade, we were told one Monday morning that a classmate (whom I disliked intensely) had been killed in an accident over the weekend. I distinctly remember that I felt only satisfaction and contentment that she was gone — meaning out of my universe, of which I was the center. I would have felt exactly the same had she moved to the next county.

Now, however, our children roll their eyes and giggle at good ol' Mom, whose voice gets all quivery whenever I'm reading a story to them and some fair child is spared from what had appeared to be his certain demise (or, worse yet, when he or his dear mother, etc., does die). Even the death of a fictional character of a few pages' acquaintance brings tears to me, and the pain is much more real when we hear of the passing of a child of whom we had some real, relational knowledge.

I think of times gone by, when it was not uncommon for half of one's children to die in childhood. As you mention in the text, modern medicine has made the death of a child a rather rare occurence in our American culture (though not throughout the world). It seems to me that our insulation from this most overwhelming personal experience has caused us, as a society and as individuals, to be able to keep at arm's length the issues of a child's need for salvation, for the present, not future, need to love God with his whole heart, mind, soul, and strength. For we do want that precious child, whenever he arrives in the presence of God, to eagerly run with bright eyes into His arms, not cower in fear or stand aside, asking "Who are you?" I do believe our brothers and sisters of other times would have much to teach us about such things, don't you?

Love, Steph

P.S. I really appreciate the quotes that you bring from other people, especially the older sources that are difficult for those of us who are not familiar with their style of English. We would miss so many rich insights from these great preachers and teachers if you did not bring them to our attention. The gems that you offer are worth the digging!

(*Continued from page 50*)   Or, *imagine your child in hell.* You have watched him cry, you have tried to comfort him in suffering, you have shed tears of sorrow yourself for him in pain. Picture him, though, in eternal misery. Will that horrible thought incite you to your knees?

There is no guarantee that, just because he is young, he will live to see tomorrow. What is most crucial for you to pray for him today? *Is he prepared to meet God?*

People who lose a child always think about how they treated the child, and what they would do differently for him, were they given just one more chance, a little more time. Consider then, that, for all intents and purposes, God is giving you another day with your child.

But you might not have tomorrow. Proverbs says:

Proverbs 27:1 Do not boast about tomorrow, for you do not know what a day will bring forth.

This is a very sobering verse, when it comes to the discipleship of our children. What is most important for my child *today?* I don't know if I'll have even tomorrow!

So, pray as though this were the last day of your child's life, and think about what you would have done differently for him. Ask yourself, "Have I done ALL I COULD to pursue his everlasting good?" And then, start doing it TODAY, if you still have the chance.

FRIDAY

5. **Pray for your child as though his ETERNAL HAPPINESS depended totally on your prayer.** If you believe that your child is in danger of hell, and that God is his only hope in escaping it, then sow with tears for him in prayer. If the house is on fire, you take great pains to get your child out. He is in a burning "building" and in mortal danger. Prayer is taking your child, who is suffering from a mortal spiritual disease, to God's hospital for treatment. And you know that, if you do not take him for treatment, he will *die without that treatment.* Is the *absolutely necessary* ingredient for your child's salvation the grace of God? Is a spiritual resurrection his only hope? Only Jesus can heal, and bring back from death (Matthew 9:18-26, etc.). Do you really love your child? Then you will not neglect prayer for that child's eternal interests.

And, once again, think about your child's ETERNAL well-being. In your prayers for your child, think about how much of your prayer is devoted to eternal things. *Do we spend the bulk of our prayer time on issues in our child's life that will not matter in 100 years* (or, a million years)? Are you more concerned about his physical health, his future success in his job, his earthly relationships, his happiness here, than about the eternal state of his soul?

Again, is the absolutely necessary ingredient for your child's salvation the grace of God? Is not a spiritual resurrection his only hope? And, is not the gospel the power of God unto salvation for all who believe (Romans 1:16)?

To the world the gospel doesn't look like power at all. It looks like weakness — asking people to be like children and telling them to depend on Jesus, instead of standing on their own two feet. But for those who believe, it is the power of God to give sinners everlasting glory.

John Piper, *Future Grace* (Sisters, Oregon: Multnomah, 1995), p. 135

Is not prayer the means through which we take hold of God's power? Then think about how much the eternal happiness of our beloved children rides on our prayer for them!

Before we leave this crucial theme, we need to be reminded that we must do more than pray, even though we can do nothing until we have prayed. Meditate on these words:

> Beware of that miserable delusion into which some have fallen, — that parents can do nothing for their children, that you must leave them alone, wait for grace, and sit still....the devil rejoices to see such reasoning, just as he always does over anything which seems to excuse indolence, or to encourage neglect of means.
>
> I know that you cannot convert your child. I know well that they who are born again are born, not of the will of man, but of God. But I know also that God says expressly, 'Train up a child in the way he should go,' and that He never laid a command on man which He would not give man grace to perform. And I know, too, that our duty is not to stand still and dispute, but to go forward and obey. It is just in the going forward that God will meet us. The path of obedience is the way in which He gives the blessing. We have only to do as the servants were commanded at the marriage feast in Cana, to fill the water-pots with water, and we may safely leave it to the Lord to turn that water into wine.
>
> J. C. Ryle, *"Train Up A Child In The Way He Should Go" (The Duties of Parents)*, pp. 7-8

> "'No one can, without renouncing the world, in the most literal sense, observe my method; and there are few, if any that would entirely devote above twenty years of the prime of life in hopes to save the souls of their children, which they think may be saved without so much ado...'[Susanna Wesley]."
>
> William and Colleen Dedrick, *The Little Book of Christian Character and Manners* (Elkton, MD: Holly Hall Publishing, 1997), p. 61

6. Pray for your child now as though he has already "gone off the deep end." This is with the understanding that, unless God yields to your pleas to Him for your child's spiritual life, your child WILL stray, he WILL depart the faith, he WILL bring the wrath of God upon himself. Therefore, imagine your son or daughter away from your holy influence, away from the Lord, lost forever, and pray now for him, that the Lord would graciously work for his good and salvation. Pour your heart out for him now, while he is still under your roof, and while you still have some influence over him. Do not wait for him to actually slip away; pray *as though he already has.* Many Christian parents feel the pain, after their grown children have actually strayed from the faith, of knowing that they did not pray this way while their children were still young. Also, if you think of your child this way, you will pray all the more fervently and will also be more diligent in his upbringing while you still have him.

And, finally ***keep always in mind the dire consequences for a home that neglects the duty of prayer.***

> Prayerless parents have cause to tremble. God's anger may light upon them in their parental relation, as Eli's neglect was visited [1 Samuel 3:13]. They have no right to expect parental happiness. They place themselves and their household in the defenceless condition of the heathen....
>
> James W. Alexander, *Thoughts on Family-Worship* (Ligonier, PA: Soli Deo Gloria Publications, 1990 [originally 1847]), pp. 55-56

Today we will wrap up our week by considering some important thoughts surrounding the issue of prayer for children. This is given in the form of an "additional note" because it *supplements* what has already been considered in this study. The wise parent, whatever his present theological leaning on children and salvation, will soberly give attention to these words.

SATURDAY

ADDITIONAL NOTE:
THE REAL REASON WHY MANY PARENTS ARE NEGLIGENT IN PRAYING FOR THEIR CHILDREN'S SALVATION

Do we *really* believe that, if they died today, our children would go to hell if they lack God's grace? Many parents are reluctant to teach and warn their children about hell, and so will not make prayer for God to save them a priority. Some, no doubt, are confident that their children are not in danger of hell until the so-called "age of accountability." Certainly it is true that God can be merciful and save whom He wants. And certainly no one wants to think that ones so "innocent" as children seem to be would be thrown into hell (innocent on the *surface*, that is, and *sometimes...*). But the Scriptures describe children as sinners, and we all see that they are subject to the outward sign of sin (death), and that they manifest the effects of sin in their behavior. And, does not God hate sin against His glory, and promise to pour out His wrath on all who hold His glory in contempt? Do not assume that, because they are children, they are therefore not in danger of hell. If we take the Scriptures as they are written, we must understand that children, as well as everyone else, *must be born again.*

Of course, as we pray for God's blessing on our child, we must also apply a warning to our children of the danger they are in as long as they remain unrepentant. Do we warn our children of this danger? Perhaps we, like many in the church today, emphasize *only God's love* for our children, and *avoid the warnings* until they are older. Jonathan Edwards preached the following to his generation, and it is just as true today:

> What has more especially given offense to many, and raised a loud cry against some preachers, as though their conduct were intolerable, is their frightening poor innocent children with talk of hell-fire, and eternal damnation. But if those who complain so loudly of this, really believe what is the general profession of the country, *viz.* That all are by nature the children of wrath, and heirs of hell — and that every one that has not been born again, whether he be young or old, is exposed every moment to eternal destruction — then such a complaint and cry as this betrays a great deal of weakness and inconsideration. Innocent as children seem to us, yet, if they are out of Christ, they are not so in the sight of God; but are in a most miserable condition, as well as grown persons...and need much to awaken them. Why should we conceal the truth from them? Will those children who have

been dealt tenderly with in this respect, and lived and died insensible of their misery till they come to feel it in hell, ever thank parents and others for their tenderness, in not letting them know their danger? If parents' love towards their children were not blind, it would affect them much more to see their children every day exposed to eternal burnings, and yet senseless, than to see them suffer the distress of that awakening which is necessary in order to their escape, and that tends to their being eternally happy as the children of God. A child that has a dangerous wound may need the painful lance [scalpel], as well as grown persons; and that would be a foolish pity, in such a case, that should hold back the lance, and throw away the life — I have seen the happy effects of dealing plainly and thoroughly with children in the concerns of their souls, without sparing them at all, in many instances; and never knew any ill consequence of it, in any one instance.

Jonathan Edwards, *Works*, vol. One, p. 393

Many parents do believe that their child is in danger of hell, but do not want to scare the child with such a horrible thought. But it is not cruel or inappropriate to warn children of the danger of hell, any more than it is to warn them about any other danger. So it is folly, as well as tragic, to avoid warning children of hell. No one complains when a tag is attached to an electric hair dryer which says, "**WARN CHILDREN OF THE RISK OF DEATH BY ELECTRIC SHOCK**," saying that children are too young to understand electricity and therefore are in no danger. No one protests warning children of the risk of abduction by strangers, for fear that the child may have nightmares. But MANY are very upset when we warn a child of the **RISK OF *ETERNAL* DEATH** for their sin against God. It scares the child, we are told. But should we not warn a child who is in danger, hoping that he will be frightened away from that danger to safety?

...If any of you that are heads of families, saw one of your children in a house that was all on fire over its head, and in eminent danger of being soon consumed in the flames, that seemed to be very insensible of its danger, and neglected to escape, after you had often spake to it, and called to it, would you go on to speak to it only in a cold and indifferent manner? Would not you cry aloud, and call earnestly to it, and represent the danger it was in, and its own folly in delaying, in the most lively manner you were capable of? Would not nature itself teach this, and oblige you to it? If you should continue to speak to it only in a cold manner, as you are wont to do in ordinary conversation about indifferent matters, would not those about you begin to think you were bereft of reason yourself? ...

If [then] we who have the care of souls, knew what hell was, had seen the state of the damned, or by any other means, become sensible how dreadful their case was...and saw our hearers in eminent danger, and that they were not sensible of their danger...it would be morally impossible for us to avoid abundantly and most earnestly setting before them the dreadfulness of that misery they were in danger of...and warning them to fly from it, and even to cry aloud to them.

Jonathan Edwards, *The Great Awakening*, ed. C. Goen, *The Works of Jonathan Edwards*
(New Haven: Yale University Press, 1972), 4:272.

We love our children, and would sooner die ourselves than to see them suffer loss when we can do something which may prevent it. Why then don't we warn our children about hell? Perhaps we don't really believe our child's spiritual house is on fire.

...Children are much more likely to believe their parents, pastors, and friends than when they become older; except perhaps, when they are on their deathbeds (when it's often too late to seek God).

Why, then, do so many vehemently oppose frightening children? They don't. They scare children away from fire, from electric sockets, from poisonous drinks or pills, from snakes, from certain toys, from anything that threatens them.

Why, then, do almost all seem to oppose frightening children with hell? The answer is obvious: they wrongly fancy that children are not in danger of hell. Can you imagine that a mother who would give her own life to save her child's wouldn't do everything to save her child from hell if she knew there was any danger?

John Gerstner, *Repent or Perish* (Morgan, PA: Soli Deo Gloria, 1990), pp. 22-23

Or, if we do believe the teaching that our children are in imminent danger, we feel that we will always have tomorrow. Maybe we will have tomorrow, and maybe many tomorrows. But, then again, maybe we won't have *even one more* tomorrow. How do we know that we have even one more day to pray for our children and deal tenderly and firmly with them concerning their sin and need of salvation? Children die all the time, as well as older people, and then the opportunity is gone forever. Let us consider once again this sobering assertion from the Proverbs, which should always be in the thinking of the conscientious parent:

Proverbs 27:1   Do not boast about tomorrow, for you do not know what a day may bring forth.

If you believe that your child is in danger of hell, and that God is his only hope in escaping it, then sow with tears for him in prayer. Once again, if the house is on fire, you take great pains to get your child out! He is in a burning "building" and in mortal danger!! To think in another way, prayer is taking your child, who is suffering from a mortal spiritual disease, to God's hospital for treatment, or he'll die. If you "stay home," and neglect to go to God, your child will die. Is the absolutely necessary ingredient for your child's salvation the grace of God? If so, then you must make prayer for your child a greater priority than anything else. Only Jesus can heal and bring back from death (Matthew 9:18-26, etc.). We will then tirelessly call upon His Name in prayer for our child.

As we close our second week considering the duty of prayer for our child, let us reflect on the dread subject of **tragedy** in this sinful and fallen world. For a parent who loves his child, the worst thought is that of *tragedy* in his child's life. We do not want our child to fall victim to tragedy. What is the worst possible tragedy that could befall our child? A devatstating injury or disease, which maims or cripples or leads to death? A crushing failure in his life? A broken relationship? As Christians, of course, as we have been reminded in these pages, the *absolute worst* tragedy that could befall our child would be to die without Christ. If our child remains nonrepentant, *everything* (whether good or bad) that happens to him is a tragedy. But for a true believer, according to Romans 8:28, there is *no such thing as a tragedy*, in the final analysis. His sins have been taken away, his relationship with his heavenly Fater has been restored in Christ, and God has ordained that in *all things,* no matter how severe and painful and tragic, *He will work for the good of that Christian.* So, let us meditate on these ***encouraging thoughts*** as we close, and labor and pray to the end that our children would be safe from harm and tragedy now and forever, and the possessors of ***unspeakable joy*** in the presence of the Father. ◯

A Note from Stephanie...

Tim,

I can just imagine all the parents gasping for air after reading what you've just written in the text. "Whoa! Heavy stuff! I've never heard _that_ before! (And, I'm not sure what I _think_ of it _now!_)"

Many will no doubt want to read over Saturday's material again to see just how Biblical and reasonable it is — I am convinced that they will certainly be compelled by what is opened up to them, even if it is unfamiliar and difficult at first encounter.

I find myself convicted — again — of the absolute necessity of getting down on my knees for our children's salvation and perseverance in the faith. We see encouraging signs of spiritual life in them and then we relax — are we _crazy?_ God help me to pray and to speak with them about _all_ of the _truth!_

Love, Stephanie

Dear Stephanie,

As I was going through some family photos, I came across this intriguing picture from several years ago. I can't help smiling as I remember that "dress-up" time. Are our children really "little _angels_"?

You've heard my Dad call our children (lovingly, I trust) "little _monsters_." I ask him, "Don't you think they're _cute_?" He answers, "Sure, but they _grow up_!" (I'm not sure how to take that . . . .)

Remember when we attended a conference when Keith was a baby? Keith started crying like crazy, so we took him off into an empty room. After the session was over, the conference speaker, R. C. Sproul, happened to walk through that room. He took one look at our wailing Keith and said, "Total depravity!"

Our children are, at once, the most precious things imaginable, and also infinitely obnoxious, perfectly self-centered, rebellious, sin-prone "little monsters"! Am I right?!

The Bible says that God always judges sin. Of course, the God we worship is merciful, and a God of love; He may save whom He wishes. Yet a sobering truth is that God is not _obligated_ to save our children.

Would God save our children if they died today? Since we are Christians, we will continually pray for God's mercy for our children. And, if our children are saved, it is not because they are innocent or precious or cute, but because of His _grace_. Then, let us pray!!

Love, Tim

Personal Meeting Time:

THE WORD

The Word Preached / Taught

Scripture Reading

Personal Reading / Study

SUNDAY

Sermon / teaching:

Scripture reading:

Personal reading / study:

Items for Prayer

MONDAY

Scripture reading: Num 6:22-27; Matt 19:13; Ps 51:5; Rom 3:23, 8:15; 1 John 3:8-12; John 8:42-43; Gen 12:1; Josh 24:2; Gal 4:4-5; Eph 1:5

Personal reading / study:

Items for Prayer

TUESDAY

Scripture reading: Proverbs 27:1; Lamentations 2:19; see Isaiah 66:7-11; reflect on the quotes on page 46

Personal reading / study:

Items for Prayer

WEDNESDAY

Scripture reading: Meditate on the passages that we have already considered this week; reflect on the quotes on pages 49-50

Personal reading / study:

Items for Prayer

THURSDAY

Scripture reading: Ezek 11:19 Deut 30:6; Eph 2:1-5; 2 Cor 4:6; 2 Tim 2:25-26; Acts 16:14; Ezek 36:27; Prov 27:1

Personal reading / study:

Items for Prayer

FRIDAY

Scripture reading: Matthew 9:18-26; 1 Samuel 3:13

Personal reading / study:

Items for Prayer

SATURDAY

Scripture reading: Proverbs 27:1; reflect on the quotes on pages 55-57

Personal reading / study:

Items for Prayer

Week 2 - SUMMARY SHEET
GUIDING QUESTIONS

[**NOTE:** *These questions, which are to be answered in the spaces below, are to guide you in reflecting on each day's content.* **All** *of the questions will not be answered* **every** *day, but only those that are helpful in processing a particular day's material.*]

1. In what specific ways has my thinking and practice been challenged or transformed by my interaction with today's biblical teaching? What particular teaching will require further study and reflection?
2. For what specific wrong thinking, sinful priorities, or areas of neglect in my responsibility, must I make confession and seek the forgiveness of the Lord?
3. Seeing that I am now responsible to strive to make the Word I have received today a reality in my life, what specifically must I do in response to God? How specifically will my life and relationships be different as a result of my time with God today? What vows might I make to the Lord this Sunday regarding my intentions to be faithful to Him in particular areas? And, seeing that, in order for this life change to become a reality, God must powerfully work by His grace and through His Spirit in my life, what specifically must I ask God to do or provide?
4. Upon what particular Bible verses will I meditate throughout the day? What verses do I desire to post in a conspicuous place to remind me to meditate upon them? What verses will I commit to memory?

MONDAY

TUESDAY

WEDNESDAY

THURSDAY

FRIDAY

SATURDAY

PRAYER FOR MY CHILD

EXPLANATION
WEEK 3

This third week in our study will build on the previous weeks' study. This week we will round out our prayer regimen for our children.

MONDAY

4. Prayer for this child's spiritual and physical protection (from spiritual and physical harm, kidnapping, abuse, etc.).

Our fourth request is a prayer for our child's protection. We are very concerned as parents about the safety of our children. This request includes prayer for physical safety at home, during play, while riding in the car, or anyplace. Also, we need to pray for protection against food poisoning, from improperly prepared or diseased food. These days there seems to be more danger of our meats (or even vegetables) being infected by harmful or fatal bacteria than there was twenty years ago. Probably the greatest fear parents have is that their child will be kidnapped. Usually we think about someone snatching our child off the playground, or even out of our back yard at home. We certainly need to pray for the Lord's protection against this. Finally, we need to pray for God's protection against abuse of our children, which can happen so easily even when we are very careful. The sexual, physical, or emotional abuse of children can produce scars that last a lifetime.

An even greater danger to the well-being of our children is the ever-present threat of *spiritual* harm, kidnapping, or abuse. This type of danger poses a threat to our child's *eternal* well-being. Are we constantly aware of our child's vulnerability to spiritual danger, and do we keep him in prayer for God's protection? Our children are just as vulnerable to spiritual dangers (such as poisonous teachings that would destroy their spiritual life, or temptations, or spiritual "kidnapping") as to physical dangers, and yet so few Christian parents seem to be aware of the spiritual threat.

What Satan desires is to "kidnap" your children, to lure them away from you and your Father's house, and harm and abuse them spiritually. That makes *physical* kidnapping by a mere man, who has limited capacity for harming your child, as horrible as that is, sound like "child's play." [This is certainly not to downplay the horror and tragedy of physical kidnapping; we would never minimize the importance of the physical safety and well-being of our children. What we are focusing on here is the *eternal* threat of spiritual kidnapping as opposed to the consequences of physical kidnapping as it affects *this temporal* life.]

Our modern assumption is that, since the child is unable to use the sword of the Spirit (i.e. he's too young to "do" the things necessary to please God or call upon God), then he is not in danger. But, *if we understand that the created world is a PICTURE of spiritual reality, we will see the fallacy of this reasoning.* Sometimes we have to protect our family from physical harm. Just because the child cannot yet defend himself, does NOT mean he is therefore not yet in danger of harm or death. If someone attacks my child, I pull out my sword (as it were) and come to his defense. Otherwise, he will certainly be overcome and taken captive or hurt or killed. If a person cannot defend himself, we do not therefore think he is not in danger; rather, *we come to his aid.* This picture points to spiritual truths concerning our children.

Satan is the enemy of our child's good, and he roams around looking for someone to devour (1 Peter 5:8). We know that the weakest victims are his desired prey.

Our point is this: **If God is not called upon to protect the child, the child will be helpless and exposed.** This is what we are saying.

Pray for God's protection. Pray for shelter from the storm, protection from the elements. You wouldn't think of letting your child remain exposed in a storm; have you provided for his spiritual protection?

God has given you the responsibility to protect your child, using all appropriate means at your disposal. For *spiritual* protection, karate moves and commando weapons will be of no use. But the Word of God and prayer are mighty weapons for our defense. Let us keep the defenses up for the protection of our family.

Train your children early to trust and call upon a strong and able and compassionate Savior, even as they would have rested in your strength and protection from physical harm. A strong parent who comes to the rescue is a great picture of the strong arm of the Lord in rescuing us from all harm.

> When I lost my footing as a little boy in the undertow at Daytona Beach, I felt as if I were going to be dragged to the middle of the ocean in an instant. It was a terrifying thing. I tried to get my bearings and figure out which way was up. But I couldn't get my feet on the ground and the current was too strong to swim. I wasn't a good swimmer anyway. In my panic I thought of only one thing: Could someone help me? But I couldn't even call out from under the water. When I felt my father's hand take hold of my upper arm like a mighty vice grip, it was the sweetest feeling in the world. I yielded entirely to being overpowered by his strength. I reveled in being picked up at his will. I did not resist. The thought did not enter my mind that I should try to show that things aren't so bad; or that I should add my strength to my Dad's arm. All I thought was, Yes! I need you! I thank you! I love your strength! I love your initiative! I love your grip! You are great! In that spirit of yielded affection one cannot boast. I call that yielded affection "faith." And my father was the embodiment of the future grace that I craved under the water. This is the faith that magnifies grace.
>
> John Piper, *Future Grace*, p. 187

The father, of course, is to be a *powerful picture* to the child of the strength of his heavenly Father. But this earthly father is not to be his protection and rescuer in the ultimate sense. In the area of his most serious vulnerability, a human father cannot come to his rescue. So, make sure this request is not neglected in your regular regimen of prayer for your children. ◇

5. Prayer for this child's perseverance in faith throughout his life, for God's continued care for his needs should I not survive to see him grown. Prayer for his future marriage partner, etc.

TUESDAY

This fifth request is very straightforward and needs little explanation (see the INTRODUCTION, on page 14). In order to reach his final home, a person must persevere in faith. And, of course, the perseverance is a gift from God. *We are praying that God would provide the grace that will enable the child to hold on by faith until the end of his life.* Has your child come to a childlike faith in the Lord for salvation? Pray that his faith would last, especially after he leaves your house and your influence. This is a very important aspect of our prayer for our children. Develop a habit of praying for his steadfast faith, and continue to pray for that in the years ahead.

God is absolutely necessary for a person's perseverance in faith. We cannot depend on the arm of the flesh for our eternal safety, and not even on the strength of our faith. Remember the incident with Peter, just before he betrayed Jesus. Jesus shattered Peter's confidence and assured him of the power available to strengthen him and preserve him upon his return:

> Luke 22:31   "Simon, Simon, behold, Satan has demanded permission to sift you like wheat; but I have prayed for you, that your faith may not fail; and you, when once you have turned again, strengthen your brothers."

In this important passage, the one thing that Jesus cites that is calculated to prevent Peter from falling totally and finally is Jesus' prayer for him. In other words, God's grace is the reality that preserves faith to the end.

Of course, this prayer is looking to God for grace for your child in his *later* life, but do not forget to seek God's enabling for your child's *present* life. It is fitting that he learn to trust when trusting comes most naturally. Do not assume that, because he is a child, he therefore is incapable of faith. Reflect on the words of H. Clay Trumbull, which bring to light the Scriptural teaching on this:

> With this knowledge of Jesus as God's representative, a child can be trained to trust Jesus at all times; to feel safe in darkness and in danger because of His nearness, His love, and His power; to be sure of His sympathy, and to rest on Him as a sufficient Saviour. That a child is capable of such faith as this, is not fairly a question. The only question, if question there be, is whether anyone but a child can attain to such faith. One thing is as sure as the words of Jesus are true, and that is, that "whosoever shall not receive the kingdom of God as a little child shall in no wise enter therein"; or, in other words, that a little child's faith is a pattern for the believers of every age.
>
> H. Clay Trumbull, *Hints on Child Training*
> (Eugene, Oregon: Great Expectations Book Company, originally published 1890), p. 79

An important element in this prayer, as well, pertains to the need for God's care of my child if I should not live to see him grown. We have all heard of the thoughtless parent who dies without having provided beforehand for his family's needs in the event of his death. What about the *spiritual* needs of his family? A wise and caring parent will entrust his children's future needs to the Provider, and ask for His continued care even beyond his own lifetime.

This is also an opportunity to pray for the child's spiritual well-being after the child is grown. We will pray for the child's future marriage partner, etc. Do not miss this opportunity, if you love your child. ⬭

WEDNESDAY

> **6. Prayer on behalf of this child for grace for his spiritual life in the following areas...**

The greatest need of your child for his life of faith, is GRACE. Without grace he will fall. If God doesn't grant your child His grace, your child is doomed. Do you believe this? This portion of the prayer sheet is a "make-or-break" section for your child's spiritual life and godliness. If your prayer is negligible or non-existent in this area, and if your child fails to pray for grace for his own life, there is little hope for his spiritual health and vitality. We will consider each of the different areas of prayer.

-Prayer of confession of specific sins which he has committed, prayer for pardon, and for his spiritual healing and restoration by faith. Confession of my own sins as though they were my child's sins. Prayer for my child concerning tendencies in myself and in my spouse that may be passed on to our child (i.e., depression, abuse, slothfulness, etc.)

The prayer for forgiveness for my child's actual sins is a very pivotal but much neglected aspect of a child's spiritual care. Usually the child does not engage in confession and prayer for pardon, except in the context of a spanking for an overt sin. But there must be a serious dealing with sin for spiritual life and health. The rule is that, if the child cannot confess his own sins, the parent prays on behalf of the child. The Lord is called upon for mercy on behalf of the child, even as the parent would call upon God for his own forgiveness. Of course, we should train the child to confess and ask forgiveness; until he does that adequately on his own, the parent plays an important role in this.

Sin is the enemy of my child's well-being in this life and, if allowed to remain in him, the destroyer of his happiness in the next life. As I carry my child to the physician when he is ill, so

also I carry my child in the arms of prayer to the Lord for the treatment of *spiritual* health-destroying ailments. The gospels have many examples of people coming to Jesus with requests that Jesus heal their children: Matthew 9:18-26 (a dead girl); Matthew 15:21ff (demon possession); Matthew 17:14-20 (epileptic boy; lack of faith); etc. So also, we are to carry our children to Jesus for healing of the diseases of their souls.

Some churches and professing believers today *deny* that children are born sinners. Dr. J. Gresham Machen recounts an experience he had listening to a sermon while visiting a typical "modern church."

> There are two notions about the teaching of children in the Church, he said. According to one notion, the children are to be told that they are sinners and need a Savior. That is the old notion, he said; it has been abandoned in the modern Church. According to the other notion, he said, which is of course the notion that we moderns hold, the business of the teacher is to nurture the tender plant of the religious nature of the child in order that it may bear fruit in a normal and healthy religious life. Was that preacher right, or was what he designated as the old notion right? Are children born good, or are they born bad? Do they need, in order that they may grow up into Christian manhood, merely the use of the resources planted in them at birth, or do they need a new birth and a divine Savior?
>
> J. Gresham Machen, *The Christian View of Man* (Edinburgh: Banner of Truth 1984), pp. 196-97

Machen's answer is the Bible's answer, that we need a new birth and a divine Savior. The Scriptures say that people in this fallen world are sinners from birth (Psalm 51:5), and that they need a Savior from birth. It is never too early to be dealing with their sin before the Lord.

Next, we are to confess our own sins. Why confess *my own* sin? What does that have to do with prayer for my child? This is necessary simply because the Scripture says that the sin of the father is passed down to subsequent generations. See, for instance, Exodus 34:

> Exodus 34:7 "[The LORD,] who keeps lovingkindness for thousands, who forgives iniquity, transgression and sin; yet He will by no means leave the guilty unpunished, visiting the iniquity of fathers on the children and on the grandchildren to the third and fourth generations."

In the Scripture there is a direct relationship between the parent's personal faithfulness and the spiritual well-being of the whole family. The obedience of a father brings blessing to his family, whereas the unfaithfulness of a father brings harm on his family. There are important examples in the Scriptures of children receiving blessing whose fathers (or forefathers) had been faithful and obedient to the Lord in their own lives (see these passages, *which are written out in this workbook following this week's studies* [pages 83-84]: Numbers 25:11-13; Psalm 106:24-31; Deuteronomy 1:35-36; 4:39-40; 5:29; 30:19-20; Psalm 37:25-29; Proverbs 20:7; Isaiah 54:13; Hebrews 11:7). There are also other passages, however, where the unfaithfulness of the parent brings harm on his family (see these passages, *which are also written out in this workbook following this week's studies* [page 84]: Exodus 34:6-7; Joshua 7:24-26; 1 Samuel 3:11-14; Psalm 106:24-27; Jeremiah 2:9; Jeremiah 32:18; Hosea 4:6).

The unavoidable implication of such sad passages as these latter ones is that, if I allow myself to indulge in *any sin*, I can expect that my children will suffer bad consequences from it. Does

this mean that my children will be punished for my sin? No, not in the sense that they are guilty personally for someone else's sins. But YES, in the sense that the sins of the father are "visited upon them." This means, for one thing, that the child will suffer the *consequences* of the parent's sin (everyone in the family suffers from the sin of a wicked father). But it also means that the sin of the father will be the child's in the sense of the child's adopting the father's sin in his own life. The sin of the father, in that sense, becomes the child's in the child's *actually committing the sin for himself.* So, the child suffers the consequences of the father's sin, and suffers from the sin being *passed on* to him like a genetically transmitted disease.

Therefore, as we are praying for our children's sins, let us not forget that *it is just as important to deal with our own sin*, even as if it was, for all intents and purposes, *our children's sin* (it will become their sin if we as parents do not deal with it in our own lives). And, while we're at it, let us not only pray, but make sure our lives do not provide a *visible bad example*.

The related responsibility is the *positive spiritual nurture* of our children in general. We give attention to their physical and temporal needs; do we neglect their spiritual and eternal needs? Listen to the warning of Jonathan Edwards regarding the dire consequences of the neglect of our children's nurture for them and ourselves:

> ...There are many who contribute to their own children's damnation, by neglecting their education, by setting them bad examples, and bringing them up in sinful ways. They take some care of their bodies, but take little care of their poor souls; they provide for them bread to eat, but deny them the bread of life, that their famishing souls stand in need of. And are there no such parents here who have thus treated their children? If their children be not gone to hell, no thanks to them; it is not because they have not done what has tended to their destruction. Seeing therefore you have had no more regard to others' salvation and have promoted their damnation, how justly might God leave you to perish yourself!
>
> Jonathan Edwards, *Works*, vol. One, p. 678

We will also take the opportunity to pray that the Lord would work graciously in our child's

THURSDAY

life to prevent the sad effects of tendencies in our own lives for ill that may be passed down to our children. ◇

The next several sections are fairly self-explanatory, but we nevertheless will say a few words here. We need to be very diligent in praying for these things for our children. We know that *these graces do not come naturally, but must be granted by God's Spirit*:

-Prayer for grace for my child to love God with all his heart, soul, mind and strength, and his neighbor as himself (Matthew 22:37-40).

This is a very pivotal prayer for a child's life of faith. That is true because God's work of sanctification in us is a matter of weaning us from love for this world and the things of this world, and working in us to love Him more and more (see the prayer request below about this). To love God with *ALL OUR BEING* is the greatest commandment, Jesus says (Matthew 22:37-40). This commandment is the *ultimate* commandment, and all other commandments are subservient to this one. That is what Jesus is saying when He calls this the *greatest* commandment. And, in doing so, Jesus has in mind that God is in a category all by Himself. We are not to love God with part, or even most, of our hearts or souls or minds or strength. And, we are not to love anything else along with Him. *He commands our all.* Listen to the psalmist:

Psalm 73:25   Whom have I in heaven but you? And earth has nothing I desire besides you. (NIV)

It must be *all*, because God, being infinitely valuable and supremely glorious and lovely, is *alone worthy* of all. It is astounding that Christians seem to think they can reserve love in their heart for created things. It is even more astounding that we can ask God to make us happy by giving us things (like earthly relationships and health and material things). It is like "marrying God for His money." Do we desire God Himself (like the psalmist that we just heard from), or His gifts? Jesus is saying that it is *God alone* Who can satisfy us and fill us with joy forever. Therefore, we are to love Him with *all*.

Do we purposefully nurture this love for God in our children? Do we strive to make God Himself special to our children? After all, it is a commandment; and, it is the *GREATEST* commandment. Do we believe that our children must obey all the commandments? What about this one? Do we nurture obedience to this, the supreme commandment, *above all*?

What, then, is to be our attitude toward people? We are to *live out* our supreme love for God by loving our neighbors *as ourselves*. The idea is that, since I am totally satisfied in God, I am freed to love others as myself. The standard Jesus gives for our love for others is the natural commitment we have to our own good. I am to regard my neighbor's best interests and needs *as though they were my own*. This is how I am to love God: by loving others in this way.

This, you see, is a different thing altogether. I am to love other people in a way that reserves my supreme love for God. It is not a proportionate matter (a percentage of our love going to God, and a percentage going to people). God is not simply to be at the top of our list of gods; He is to be our only God. We are to love other creatures (our *neighbor*) with a love that is appropriate to *another creature* (as *ourself*). No creature is worthy of *all* my heart.

The obedience of any commandment of God is dependent on His supplying the grace and power to obey. That is why we are praying for **grace** to obey these commandments.

> **-Prayer for love for God's Word, for his receiving it with glad obedience (including those commands which specifically address children, such as honoring and obeying parents).**

This prayer is pivotal in that my child must love God's Word and the obedience of it, or he cannot be a child of God. And, he will not naturally love God's Word. He must have the grace

of the Spirit to perceive the spiritual beauty in the Word. Do not neglect prayer for this.

-Prayer that God would pour out the Spirit of prayer on my child, so that he might develop a habit of prayer early, to continue for his lifetime.

Just as we direct our children in the early development of habits of daily hygiene and physical fitness, so also we lead them to develop habits of devotion. But the life and power of prayer do not come naturally to sinners. Of course, a child of God will breathe out in prayer as naturally as a newborn child will breathe out in crying. But, according to Romans 8:26, the Spirit must assist us for fervent, effective prayer. *Your child's prayer will be living and powerful if the Spirit imparts "a Spirit of prayer."*

-Prayer for grace for my child to increasingly desire spiritual pleasures and treasures, as he seeks his happiness in God, and for weaning from love of the treasures and pleasures of this world.

This request deserves special comment, since this necessary discipline of weaning from the world is so seldom taught in the church today. *One of the most important aspects of biblical discipleship is weaning our child from love for the world.* It is not surprising that, given the wealth and abundance of our lifestyle, this biblical discipline is not popular. The modern church thinks a person can grow in worldly gain and grow spiritually at the same time, in a balanced lifestyle, "as long as you're thankful." Now, thankfulness is a profoundly important response to God's gifts. But, how easy it is to fall in love with the gifts and look to them for happiness instead of God!

Jesus says, *"Do not lay up for yourselves treasures upon earth...but lay up for yourselves treasures in heaven," "Where your treasure is, there will your heart be also,"* and *"You cannot serve both God and mammon"* (Matthew 6:19-24). He says that *"desires for other things"* choke out the Word in our hearts (Mark 4:19). He says, regarding our life in this world, in John 12:25, *"He who loves his life loses it; and he who hates his life in this world shall keep it to life eternal."* John says, *"Do not love the world or the things of the world"* (1 John 2:15), and the apostle Paul says, *"set your mind on the things above, not on the things that are on earth"* (Colossians 3:2). In light of such verses, how can we encourage a love of things in our children?

One of best ways to think about the biblical teaching on the relationship between our love for God and our love for things is to think about the scales of a balance. Reflect on the words of the seventeenth century pastor and teacher, Henry Scougal:

> The love of the world, and the love of God, are like the scales of a balance, as the one falleth, the other doth rise: when our natural inclinations prosper, and the creature is exalted in our soul, religion is faint, and doth languish; but when earthly objects wither away, and lose their beauty, and the soul begins to cool and flag in its prosecution [pursuit] of them, then the seeds of grace take root, and the Divine life begins to flourish and prevail.
>
> Henry Scougal, *The Life of God in the Soul of Man*
> (Harrisonburg, VA: Spinkle Publications, 1986), p. 109

Tim,

I remember all the hours and hours (and hours) I have spent in the last 12 or so years nursing babies. I have very fond memories of those times, both when I was using the time to read to other children, and when it was just the baby and me.

The process of weaning came along fairly naturally as the children's appetite for a variety of foods and beverages increased, as well as their skill in using a cup. I would cut back to nursing morning and night only, then to once a day. In fact, it always amazed me at how small a ripple it was in their lives when that first "no nursing" day came. They would be so satisfied with what they were getting at the table that they "never looked back," so to speak.

The weaning process is different for each mother and child, but as time goes by, children _do_ leave their dependence on milk behind, being nourished and satisfied by solid food. We would find it alarming to find a six-year-old (without special challenges) drinking only milk from bottles. Would that we could observe such a common movement from dependence on the things of this world to satisfaction and pleasure in God Himself in all His children! May God use me again in _this_ weaning process, too, through prayer.

Love, Stephanie

P.S. I know you have struggled with this spiritual "weaning," Tim. Your growing up years had many memories of special gifts....and you cherish the memories! You're not a "spoil-sport," nor are you against gifts and Christmas and birthdays and celebration! There's not a "Grinch" bone in your body! But I do appreciate your emphasis that God is _so_ special, that the _most_ special joys of this world pale in comparison.

Stephanie,

Until recently, I hadn't really thought about the need to be _spiritually_ "weaned." I had thought _a lot_ about disciplining our children to put sinful desires and practices to death. Do our children also have to be "weaned" from the _good_ things of this life? You're right, Steph: this is a struggle!

It is startling that Jesus identified "the deceitfulness of riches," "the desires for other things," and "the pleasures of this life," as things which can "choke out" the Word in our lives (Mark 4:19; Luke 8:14). He mentions here, not _evil things_, but _good gifts_ that may prevent the harvest! As I meditated on this around Christmas time a while back, it hit me that, if our joy comes from hearing that our children walk in the truth, then how can we encourage the enjoyment of the very things that can prevent that very truth from taking hold in our children? We need to really think this through!

"Weaning" is such an apt picture of the spiritual truth here. That's because, when a child is weaned, he _loses interest_ in nursing in favor of solid food, which he finds to be more satisfying. It is the same in spiritual things.

I'm _not_ talking here about _abstinence_, but about _losing interest_ in the _inferior_ treasures and pleasures of this world, when our affections are transferred to _superior_, _spiritual_ joys in God and in communion with Him. It's not necessarily a matter of suppressing our desires for things, but of seeing our desires "graduated" to the _higher_ joys of the "unseen" world. It's not _taking away things_ from our children, but nurturing in them desires for the joys and pleasures of the spiritual world. When they are spiritually alive and sensitive, they start _preferring_ godliness and spiritual pursuits.

I think about the practical implications of this thinking. It seems that many Christians will find this almost impossible to practice in our materialistic, fun-loving, entertainment-oriented culture. The first weaning (physical weaning from milk to solid food) comes naturally; the second (the spiritual weaning) does not. This world and its joys are simply too visible and charming and desirable! That's why we must pray for God's grace.

Remember how we looked forward to our children being weaned? Do we have as deep a longing that they would be _spiritually_ weaned? Once again, let us _pray!!_

Love, Tim

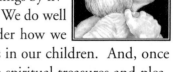

In the wealthy, materialistic, peacetime culture in which we live, this kind of discipline is almost unheard of. Do we not encourage a love of things by living such a luxurious lifestyle, to the spiritual harm of our children? We do well to very carefully examine our way of life at this point, and consider how we might encourage a weaning from the world's delights and pleasures in our children. And, once again, the grace of God's Spirit is necessary to generate love for the spiritual treasures and pleasures that are in God.

FRIDAY

> -Prayer for grace to protect this child against specific temptations which he is now fighting by faith, and the temptations which he can be expected to fight in the future.

Do we pray for our child *before* he becomes exposed to temptations? Do we labor beforehand to secure for him protection from Satan's future attacks in the teenage years? Do we make sure he has his spiritual "armor" in place, as Paul prescribes in Ephesians 6:10-20?

It is crucially important that we pray for God's grace in advance. Think also about the "normal" milestones in life, such as adolescence. Rebellion is not "normal." It is sin. Lust is not just part of growing up: it is sin and the destroyer of spiritual life. Therefore, do not neglect to pray well in advance for whatever grace you know your child will need. "Be prepared" is a good motto here.

> -Prayer for grace for dealing with present and future suffering and trials, and with his fears and sorrows.

Pray for God's grace to prepare your child for trials and suffering. It is very important to include this as a part of our regular prayer. But it is hard to keep it in mind, especially if our child is not going through any trials or suffering *right now*. Even the healthiest and most well-adjusted of children face life's dark valleys even as adults do, and so often they are totally unprepared spiritually to face them. Hope for the best, but prepare for the worst. Remember, trials and suffering are the occasions in which God works in producing godliness. The chief end for my child is NOT enjoyment of THIS life, but the enjoyment of GOD. God orders our days so as to produce spiritual gain, not to increase the comforts of this life. He sends our afflictions to increase the health of our spiritual life in Him, and to wean us from our love for this world. *We must be filled with His grace in order to withstand and thrive in times of suffering and adversity.* Consider these words of H. Clay Trumbull:

> One plain teaching of these facts concerning the sorrows of children is, that the young need the comfort and joys of a Christian faith for the life that now is, quite as surely as the aged need a Christian hope for the life that is to come. The surest way of bringing even a child to see the brighter side of

this life is by inducing him to put his trust in an omnipotent Savior, who loves him, and who makes all things work together for good to him if only he trust himself to His care and walks faithfully in His service. The invitations and the promises of the Bible are just what children need, to give them happiness and hope for now and for hereafter.

H. Clay Trumbull, *Hints on Child Training*, pp. 146-147

-Prayer for grace for purity and for humility in his life.

Do not forget to pray for the essential graces of purity and humility. Childhood is the most excellent time to cultivate godliness, and the twin graces of purity and humility are at the heart of true godliness. Do not fall prey to wrong thinking in assuming that these are not childhood virtues. We should pray for our children to be filled with purity and humility, especially when their hearts are still relatively tender and spiritual impressions can be more deeply stamped. And, do not mistakingly assume that purity and humility *come naturally* to "innocent" children. They are born sinners, and God must graciously grant them the spiritual virtues of purity and humility.

Purity of heart is essential for the enjoyment of God, for a child as well as an adult.

Psalm 73:1 Surely God is good to Israel, to those who are pure in heart.

Matthew 5:8 Blessed are the pure in heart, for they will see God.

If you truly want your children to be happy, then, *pray for purity of heart.* Psalm 73:1 promises God's goodness extended to the pure in heart, and Jesus in Matthew 5:8 says that the pure in heart are blessed, for they shall enjoy the spiritual sight of the glory and beauty and excellence of the living God. To "behold [Jesus'] glory" (John 17:24) is what happiness is all about. For the Christian, this is happiness, complete and eternal!

Humility is a virtue God honors, and the contrite and lowly heart is the one God "esteems."

Isaiah 66:2 "This is the one I esteem: he who is humble and contrite in spirit,
and trembles at my word." (NIV)

If we want our children to be *truly* built up, to be *truly* esteemed, to be *truly* honored, pray for the grace of *humility* in the sight of God and man to be built into them.

What is to be our children's attitude toward themselves and God? In these days when "self-esteem" is the popular quality many are building into their children, the Bible enjoins on us the opposite principle of "***GOD***-esteem," where valuing and assigning worth to *God* is the central and dominating concern. Today children are taught that their value is determined by how much God loves THEM, whereas the Scriptures speak of our virtue as being determined by what WE love. Instead of focusing on myself, and how much God loves me, my worth is determined by whether I love and cherish God above all things. At the center of the Christian faith is *MY LOVE FOR GOD*, who in His excellence and spiritual beauty and majesty is infinitely worthy of my deepest devotion and love and esteem. The grace of humility enables one to seek to assign value (glory) to the supremely valuable Being, God Himself. Therefore, let us pray for this essential virtue to be granted to our beloved children.

-Prayer for grace for personal ministry and usefulness (use of spiritual gifts, love in relationships, compassion for the lost, opportunities for service and sharing the gospel, school, job, etc).

Take regular time to pray for fruitfulness for your child in his life and ministry. One of the greatest robbers of joy and fruitfulness in the church is the idea that children and youth are there to be *ministered unto*, rather than to be *servants*. God has gifted and equipped young people for ministry, too. And, if a child is trained to see service as being *central and vital* to being a Christian, he will be able to serve naturally, as a habitual thing, when he reaches adulthood.

In Psalm 127:4 children are likened to "arrows in the hand of a warrior." How is our view of children to be shaped by this verse? Does not the terminology suggest that our children are to be useful in the warfare against Satan and his "kingdom"? Is not a young child of the King, who is built up in faith and love, is mighty in holiness, and is faithful in prayer, an *awesome weapon* against God's adversaries?

And, is not our great passion that the fame of Christ spread to the ends of the earth, and that His Kingdom would advance? Then we must pray that our children would be prepared for the noble purpose of extending the Kingdom of God.

Therefore, do not neglect prayer for your child in this area.

SATURDAY

-Prayer for grace to love his enemies, and for a forgiving spirit toward those who persecute or mistreat him (Matthew 5:44; Luke 6:28).

Finally, devote yourself to prayer for the Spirit's virtues of *love and forgiveness* to be granted to your child. Cultivating a pattern early of dealing with problems in relationships with a gracious and loving and forgiving spirit will immeasurably benefit your child later as he strives for a godly life. This is an area of special vulnerability for children. Many children, even from Christian families, develop a habit of harboring bitterness and a vengeful spirit toward *friends and siblings* who mistreat them.

Further, do we concern ourselves with their bitter and vengeful attitude toward their *enemies?* It is hard enough to forgive those we are predisposed to *love;* what about those who are seen as *enemies?* Further, do we desire *love*, that *positive* virtue, toward their enemies and those who treat them cruelly? It is one thing to merely *not think hateful thoughts* about someone; it is quite another to *actually love* that person! Do we cultivate love in our children for unlovely people? (By the way, what is the attitude that they see *in us* in our interactions with difficult people?) *This is where the GRACE OF GOD comes in!* Do not neglect prayer for much grace from the Lord in this vital area.

> ### 7. Prayer for his physical life and health, and for his material needs.
Our next area of prayer is one that usually has a much greater priority in prayer guides than it does on this one. That is not to say that these requests are not important. But we would assert that these requests have an importance, not as goals and desires *in themselves,* but as they *serve the higher principle of spiritual life and growth.* The Christian is to have God, and fellowship with Him, as the ultimate goal of everything he does and has. Therefore, when we pray for physical life and health, it is not because we love this life and desire to enjoy the world, but because *physical life and health are the context for serving the Lord in our body.*
This is not a matter of becoming more spiritual and less physical; God has created us as physical beings, and has redeemed our whole humanity. It is rather a matter of setting the physical aspect of our created being to work in serving God and pursuing spiritual treasures and pleasures *IN HIM.*
There are many passages that teach that this life and its concerns are fleeting and temporary, and that we should not grasp this life, but gladly set it apart for God and eternal blessings in Him.
John 12:25 "He who loves his life loses it; and he who hates his life in this world shall keep it to life eternal."
Psalm 63:3 Because your love is better than life, my lips will glorify you. (NIV)
Romans 12:1 I urge you therefore, brethren, by the mercies of God, to present your bodies a living and holy sacrifice, acceptable to God, which is your spiritual service of worship.
2 Corinthians 4:16-5:4 Therefore we do not lose heart, but though our outer man is decaying, yet our inner man is being renewed day by day. For momentary, light affliction is producing for us an eternal weight of glory far beyond all comparison, while we look not at the things which are seen, but at the things which are not seen; for the things which are seen are temporal, but the things which are not seen are eternal. For we know that if the earthly tent which is our house is torn down, we have a building from God, a house not made with hands, eternal in the heavens. For indeed in this house we groan, longing to be clothed with our dwelling from heaven; inasmuch as we, having put it on, shall not be found naked. For indeed while we are in this tent, we groan, being burdened, because we do not want to be unclothed, but to be clothed, in order that what is mortal may be swallowed up by life.
Regarding material needs, once again, the Christian will not value material things in themselves, but as valuable in serving the higher goal of joy and happiness in God.
Matthew 6:33 "But seek first His kingdom and His righteousness; and all these things shall be added to you."
Mark 4:18-19 "And others are the ones on whom seed was sown among the thorns; these are the ones who have heard the word, and the worries of the world, and the deceitfulness of riches, and the desires for other things enter in and choke the word, and it becomes unfruitful."

Matthew 6:19-24 "Do not lay up for yourselves treasures upon earth, where moth and rust destroy, and where thieves break in and steal. But lay up for yourselves treasures in heaven, where neither moth nor rust destroys, and where thieves do not break in or steal; for where your treasure is, there will your heart be also. The lamp of the body is the eye; if therefore your eye is clear, your whole body will be full of light. But if your eye is bad, your whole body will be full of darkness. If therefore the light that is in you is darkness, how great is the darkness! No one can serve two masters; for either he will hate the one and love the other, or he will hold to one and despise the other. You cannot serve God and mammon."

1 John 2:15-17 Do not love the world, nor the things in the world. If anyone loves the world, the love of the Father is not in him. For all that is in the world, the lust of the flesh and the lust of the eyes and the boastful pride of life, is not from the Father, but is from the world. And the world is passing away, and also its lusts; but the one who does the will of God abides forever.

Colossians 3:1-3 If then you have been raised up with Christ, keep seeking the things above, where Christ is, seated at the right hand of God. Set your mind on the things above, not on the things that are on earth. For you have died and your life is hidden with Christ in God.

Having said this, though, God does want us to pray for *all* of our needs to show *our dependence on Him for everything*. And, He is glorified in our looking to Him in faith for *everything*.

So, prayer for our children's physical life and material needs is a integral part of our prayer outline for our children (on this, see the *personal notes on physical needs* on pages 78-79).

> ## 8. Prayer for specific spiritual needs of this child, from the INVENTORY and EVALUATION sheets.

This final area directs us to the Worksheets that we are encouraged to fill out concerning our child. As we said at the beginning, we will introduce these sheets following this series of studies on the PRAYER FOR MY CHILD guide.

The SPIRITUAL INVENTORY WORKSHEET has a concluding section that lists specific prayer requests that have arisen as a result of the information compiled on the Worksheet. To pray for these, go to the worksheet and read them and pray for them from the sheet. This is very important because it forms a link between the evaluation of the child's spiritual state and the regular prayer time for the child. The INVENTORY sheet is designed to identify areas in need of prayer.

The SPIRITUAL PROGRESS EVALUATION WORKSHEET contains 45 heart and character traits which are to be worked on systematically, and one's progress monitored, over a period of time. As we say in the introduction to the use of that worksheet, the mastering of the traits is *dependent on the Lord and prayer to Him*. Therefore, we will take the opportunity to pray for whatever area is being worked on from the sheet.

These worksheets are designed to assist the parent in producing a "tailor-made" approach to prayer for his particular children. The personality and life-situation and needs of the people we love will affect the way we pray for them and our priorities in prayer.

Dear Tim,

Our children's physical life and health, and material needs, are so very high in our awareness as parents, aren't they? I suppose that's why it's the one "prayer request" that fills probably 90% of the prayer meetings in 90% of the churches in America. We could easily fill hours each week praying not only for recovery from illness or accident, issues relating to growing into adolescent bodies, allergies, and various physical or developmental challenges, but oh, those "material needs." When family finances allow, don't we pray to get "the right" sports equipment, band instruments, tickets to —, clothes or shoes, books, — lessons, part-time job, internship, toys, scholarship, acceptance to —, first car, bicycle, etc.. And, if finances don't allow, we pray for the income to keep them fed, clothed, and having a roof over their head. "Been there, done that," as they say.

I think when we pray for any of these things we must remember to teach what Paul said about learning to be content in plenty or in want (Philippians 4:11-12). Sometimes I feel that I hardly know any children who are able to be content — even Christopher has his grabby moments! I'll grant that our culture is working overtime against us on this score, but we really must pray vigorously for "godliness with contentment" (1 Timothy 6:6) as we pray for their material needs (that's <u>needs</u>, not <u>wants!</u>). And that contentment in this life comes only, as you say, when we are mindful that this world is not our home . . . have we and our children been stockpiling treasures in heaven? (The fight to keep their rooms clean calls that into serious question!)

Now I understand why some saints are respectfully known as prayer <u>warriors!</u> Let us take up our swords . . .

Love, Stephanie

Dear Stephanie,

We don't get to prayer for physical needs specifically until rather late in the prayer guide. Does that mean it's not important? No. We live, glorify and serve God, and will be raised at the resurrection, in the body. God wants us to pray for physical needs.

We often equate "blessing" with <u>material</u> things that the Lord provides. Or, we may say we're "blessed" with <u>physical benefits</u>, 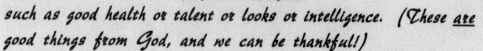 such as good health or talent or looks or intelligence. (These <u>are</u> good things from God, and we can be thankful!)

But, although we seem to most often equate "blessing" with the good things of this life and this world, Numbers 6:23-27 says blessing is a spiritual sight and enjoyment of the radiant countenance or presence of God. And Jesus Himself relates blessing to <u>spiritual</u> things in His "Beatitudes" (Matthew 5:3-12). "Blessing" is the spiritual enjoyment of God Himself.

Can we pray for things and for happiness in this world? It's one thing to (<u>rightly!</u>) ask God for everything we need; it's another thing to see God as just someone who gives us things to make us comfortable and happy in <u>this</u> world. We pray most earnestly for what we think we need most to satisfy us, or comfort us, or make us happy. It's one thing to <u>need</u> things, like daily bread, and thankfully ask God to provide them; it's quite another thing to <u>depend</u> on things for happiness!

In praying for physical things, do we pray for the things that our children will need in order to be happy <u>in God</u>, or to be happy <u>in this world</u>? We need to carefully think about this . . . and then pray for what will <u>truly</u> make our children happy.

Love, Tim

Personal Meeting Time:

THE WORD

The Word Preached / Taught

Scripture Reading

Personal Reading / Study

SUNDAY

Sermon / teaching:

Scripture reading:

Personal reading / study:

Items for Prayer

MONDAY

Scripture reading: 1 Peter 5:8; Matthew 26:41

Personal reading / study:

Items for Prayer

TUESDAY

Scripture reading: Luke 22:31

Personal reading / study:

Items for Prayer

WEDNESDAY

Scripture reading: Matthew 9:18-26; 15:21ff; 17:14-20; Psalm 51:5; Exodus 34:7; the passages on pages 83-84

Personal reading / study:

Items for Prayer

THURSDAY

Scripture reading: Matthew 22:37-40; Psalm 73:25; Romans 8:26; Matthew 6:19-24; Mark 4:19; John 12:25; 1 John 2:15; Colossians 3:2

Personal reading / study:

Items for Prayer

FRIDAY

Scripture reading: Ephesians 6:10-20; Isaiah 66:2; Psalm 73:1; Matthew 5:8; Isaiah 66:2; Matthew 5:44; Luke 6:28

Personal reading / study:

Items for Prayer

SATURDAY

Scripture reading: John 12:25; Ps 63:3; Rom 12:1; 2 Cor 4:16-5:4; Matt 6:19-24, 33; Mark 4:18-19; John 2:15-17; Col 3:1-3

Personal reading / study:

Items for Prayer

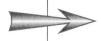

WEEK 3 - SUMMARY SHEET
GUIDING QUESTIONS

[NOTE: *These questions, which are to be answered in the spaces below, are to guide you in reflecting on each day's content.* **All** *of the questions will not be answered* **every** *day, but only those that are helpful in processing a particular day's material.*]

1. In what specific ways has my thinking and practice been challenged or transformed by my interaction with today's biblical teaching? What particular teaching will require further study and reflection?
2. For what specific wrong thinking, sinful priorities, or areas of neglect in my responsibility, must I make confession and seek the forgiveness of the Lord?
3. Seeing that I am now responsible to strive to make the Word I have received today a reality in my life, what specifically must I do in response to God? How specifically will my life and relationships be different as a result of my time with God today? What vows might I make to the Lord this Sunday regarding my intentions to be faithful to Him in particular areas? And, seeing that, in order for this life change to become a reality, God must powerfully work by His grace and through His Spirit in my life, what specifically must I ask God to do or provide?
4. Upon what particular Bible verses will I meditate throughout the day? What verses do I desire to post in a conspicuous place to remind me to meditate upon them? What verses will I commit to memory?

MONDAY

TUESDAY

WEDNESDAY

THURSDAY

FRIDAY

SATURDAY

ADDITIONAL NOTE

These are some examples in the Scriptures of *children receiving blessing whose father* **(or forefathers)** *had been faithful and obedient to the Lord in their own lives:*

Numbers 25:11-13 "Phinehas son of Eleazar, the son of Aaron, the priest, has turned my anger away from the Israelites; for he was as zealous as I am for my honor among them, so that in my zeal I did not put an end to them. Therefore tell him I am making my covenant of peace with him. He and his descendants will have a covenant of a lasting priesthood, because he was zealous for the honor of his God and made atonement for the Israelites." (NIV)

Psalm 106:24-31 Then they despised the pleasant land; they did not believe his promise.
   They grumbled in their tents and did not obey the LORD.
So he swore to them with uplifted hand that he would make them fall in the desert,
   make their descendants fall among the nations and scatter them throughout the lands.
They yoked themselves to the Baal of Peor and ate sacrifices offered to lifeless gods;
   they provoked the LORD to anger by their wicked deeds, and a plague broke out among them.
But Phinehas stood up and intervened, and the plague was checked.
   This was credited to him as righteousness for endless generations to come. (NIV)

Deuteronomy 1:35-36 "Not one of these men, this evil generation, shall see the good land which I swore to give your fathers, except Caleb the son of Jephunneh; he shall see it, and to him and to his sons I will give the land on which he has set foot, because he has followed the LORD fully."

Deuteronomy 4:39-40 "Know therefore today, and take it to your heart, that the LORD, He is God in heaven above and on the earth below; there is no other. So you shall keep His statutes and His commandments which I am giving you today, that it may go well with you and with your children after you, and that you may live long on the land which the LORD your God is giving you for all time."

Deuteronomy 5:29 "Oh that they had such a heart in them, that they would fear Me, and keep all My commandments always, that it may be well with them and with their sons forever!"

Deuteronomy 30:19-20 "I call heaven and earth to witness against you today, that I have set before you life and death, the blessing and the curse. So choose life in order that you may live, you and your descendants, by loving the LORD your God, by obeying His voice, and by holding fast to Him; for this is your life and the length of your days, that you may live in the land which the LORD swore to your fathers, to Abraham, Isaac, and Jacob, to give them."

Psalm 37:25-29 I have been young, and now I am old;
   yet I have not seen the righteous forsaken, or his descendants begging bread.
All day long he is gracious and lends; and his descendants are a blessing.
Depart from evil, and do good, so you will abide forever.
   For the LORD loves justice, and does not forsake His godly ones;
They are preserved forever; but the descendants of the wicked will be cut off.
   The righteous will inherit the land, and dwell in it forever.

Proverbs. 20:7 A righteous man who walks in his integrity — How blessed are his sons after him.

Isaiah 54:13 "And all your sons will be taught of the LORD; and the well-being of your sons will be great."

Hebrews 11:7 By faith Noah, being warned by God about things not yet seen, in reverence prepared an ark for the salvation of his household, by which he condemned the world, and became an heir of the righteousness which is according to faith.

Some passages where *the unfaithfulness of the parent brings harm on his family:*

Exodus 34:6-7 Then the LORD passed by in front of him and proclaimed, "The LORD, the LORD God, compassionate and gracious, slow to anger, and abounding in lovingkindness and truth; who keeps lovingkindness for thousands, who forgives iniquity, transgression and sin; yet He will by no means leave the guilty unpunished, visiting the iniquity of fathers on the children and on the grandchildren to the third and fourth generations."

Joshua 7:24-26 Then Joshua and all Israel with him, took Achan the son of Zerah, the silver, the mantle, the bar of gold, his sons, his daughters, his oxen, his donkeys, his sheep, his tent and all that belonged to him; and they brought them up to the valley of Achor. And Joshua said, "Why have you troubled us? The LORD will trouble you this day." And all Israel stoned them with stones; and they burned them with fire after they had stoned them with stones. And they raised over him a great heap of stones that stands to this day, and the LORD turned from the fierceness of His anger. Therefore the name of that place has been called the valley of Achor to this day.

1 Samuel 3:11-14 And the LORD said to Samuel, "Behold, I am about to do a thing in Israel at which both ears of everyone who hears it will tingle. In that day I will carry out against Eli all that I have spoken concerning his house, from beginning to end For I have told him that I am about to judge his house forever for the iniquity which he knew, because his sons brought a curse on themselves and he did not rebuke them. And therefore I have sworn to the house of Eli that the iniquity of Eli's house shall not be atoned for by sacrifice or offering forever."

Psalm 106:24-29 Then they despised the pleasant land; they did not believe his promise.
  They grumbled in their tents and did not obey the LORD.
So he swore to them with uplifted hand that he would make them fall in the desert,
  make their descendants fall among the nations and scatter them throughout the lands.
They yoked themselves to the Baal of Peor and ate sacrifices offered to lifeless gods;
  they provoked the LORD to anger by their wicked deeds, and a plague broke out among them.
(NIV)

Jeremiah 2:9 "Therefore I bring charges against you again," declares the LORD. And I will bring charges against your children's children." (NIV)

Jeremiah 32:18 You show love to thousands but bring the punishment for the fathers' sins into the laps of their children after them. O great and powerful God, whose name is the LORD Almighty, (NIV)

Hosea 4:6 My people are destroyed for lack of knowledge. Because you have rejected knowledge, I also will reject you from being My priest. Since you have forgotten the law of your God, I also will forget your children.

PART TWO

THE
SPIRITUAL
EVALUATION
WORKSHEETS

Dear Stephanie,

    In putting together these notes for the book, I've looked at a lot of photos of our children from over the years. I'm constantly amazed as I compare pictures taken of our children in the past with what I see sitting around our dinner table today! As my uncle used to say, "My, how you have grown!" It's always an exhilarating experience to watch our children grow and mature, to see their knowledge and abilities expand, and their special qualities and strengths appear.

    You mentioned in your note on love for our children that growing Christlikeness is really what causes us to delight in our children most. You said that, while non-Christians find most pleasure in the _natural_ attributes and characteristics of their children, the sweetest rejoicing in Christian parents is in _likeness to God_ seen in their children.

    The back cover of this book highlights John's words, "_I have no greater joy than to hear that my children are walking in the truth._" While John's "children" were Christians of all ages whom he had been privileged to teach, the principle is the same for parents. There is simply no greater kind of joy than this! The _most_ joy, and the _deepest_ joy, for a Christian parent, then, is when his children reflect the character of God. When God's passions are the child's passions, when the child's eyes light up at the thought of God just as much as Pooh's do at the thought of a pot of honey, then we are happy indeed!

    Surely a Christian parent may be thankful for natural abilities and accomplishments that he sees in his children. But the _sweetest joy_ that we experience in our children will come when they love what their heavenly Father loves, and value what He values, and make His glory their highest goal and strongest passion. _This_ is really why we pray!

    The second part of this book is included for just this reason. If what we desire above all things is that our children would adorn the beauty of God's character, then this will be the focus of our prayer. And, if what we love _most_ in our children is _what may be seen of Christ in them_, then our love for and joy in our children will deepen and sweeten as God works more and more Christlikeness in them.

Love, Tim

SPIRITUAL EVALUATION

INTRODUCTION

What is "SPIRITUAL EVALUATION" **all about?** It consists of two worksheets, the SPIRITUAL INVENTORY WORKSHEET and the SPIRITUAL PROGRESS EVALUATION WORKSHEET. These two worksheets are designed to assist parents in offering effective and relevant prayer on behalf of their children. The worksheets are intended to be used in conjunction with the PRAYER FOR MY CHILD guide, the last request of which directs the parent to pray for requests from these evaluation worksheets. This week you will be introduced to the thinking behind the SPIRITUAL INVENTORY WORKSHEET, and will receive instructions for its use. This teaching will be distributed over six days, with Sunday being the day of rest. Then, next week the SPIRITUAL PROGRESS EVALUATION WORKSHEET will be presented, along with its instructions. We will fill out our initial evaluation sheets for each of our sons and daughters.

We will begin by considering the picture of a child's *physical body,* and *the parent's careful attention to its health and well-being.* Parental observation of physical signs of health or sickness on his child's body is a major part of his loving care of his child. It would be a sure indication of neglect if conspicuous, observable signs of illness or injury escaped the notice of the parent, and the needed care and treatment were not provided for the child.

When our child is ill, sometimes we can resort to "home remedies," or use over-the-counter drugs or treatments that will satisfy the need. Or, when our child is injured in an accident, we assess the seriousness of the injury, and, if it is relatively minor, we can apply first aid.

But when the nature or severity of the illness appears to be beyond our ability to adequately treat it, we have to take the child to a physician, to seek a true diagnosis of the nature of the illness, and to seek proper treatment which will (hopefully) lead toward recovery and restored health. When our child is hurt in an accident, if it appears that the injury is too serious for our home treatment, we seek professional medical help.

Most parents have at least one medical resource book in their home that offers the advice of medical professionals for a variety of illnesses and injuries. Many illnesses or injuries require just common sense to treat, and minimal medical training and skills.

But every parent sees that there is often the need of the examination and treatment of the child by a medical professional or in an Emergency Room. And, no loving parent would knowingly neglect an infirmity in or injury to his child's body when treatment is available.

> *The principle to which this points is the parent's responsibility to also carefully attend to his child's spiritual needs, and to provide for the proper treatment and remedy when needed.*

It is astounding that so many parents are so scrupulously attentive to their child's *physical* needs, and seek the finest available professional help when the need requires it, yet pay relatively little attention to spiritual needs. Or, if they do notice spiritual infirmities or injuries, they seem to be so often satisfied with applying *superficial* treatments! It seems that, if a remedy makes a person "feel better," then it is hailed as a success. Whatever the case, it seems that most parents are much more attentive to their children's physical needs than their spiritual.

But *God has called us to be equally attentive to our children's spiritual needs*, and *to faithfully seek to provide the proper diagnoses and treatments for the needs that arise.*

Of course, with spiritual needs, as well as physical, parents seem comfortable in trusting their own powers of observation and knowledge and common sense and skills. In spiritual matters, do we trust in "home remedies," or do we take our children to the "Great Physician"? The point that we must make here is that ***the deepest spiritual needs of our children can only be sufficiently and lastingly treated by the Great Physician Himself!*** When it comes to the treatment of *spiritual* diseases and injuries, no "home remedies" will do. When we confidently trust in our parenting skills and wisdom and love, our children miss the *only* treatment that will heal and restore them.

Of course, as in the case with physical illnesses that require professional medical treatment, there are times when the spiritual health of our child requires the assistance of those whom God has gifted and called and equipped to be pastors and shepherds and "physicians of souls" in His church. God certainly uses such gifted individuals in His work of treating His people's spiritual health problems and diseases. But even then, we make a dire mistake if we trust in human "care providers" *alone*, and their human skills or knowledge or expertise. Many parents learn too late that the spiritual care of their children cannot be simply entrusted to a Sunday School teacher, or youth leader, or even a pastor.

But parents can also fall prey to trusting in the spiritual *means*, such as prayer, for the needs of their children. In other words, many parents trust in *their mastery and practice of spiritual principles and actions.* This is dangerous because it is a subtle form of trusting human strength and wisdom, of trusting the arm of the flesh instead of the Spirit of God. The means themselves are only the vehicle to carry us to the One who actually administers the treatment.

Only God Himself, as we carry our children to Him in prayer, can apply the life-giving, life-sustaining, life-saving remedy through His Word and Spirit.

How do we go about seeking the blessed care of the Great Physician? Stay tuned . . . .

SPIRITUAL EVALUATION

EXPLANATION

WEEK 4

Self-examination. The place to begin in seeking the care of the Great Physician is in *our own self-examination*. We cannot expect to be useful in providing spiritual health care for our children unless we first *submit ourselves* to the care and treatment of the Great Physician!

The principle of the evaluation of our children to determine their health and needs arises out of the idea of *self*-evaluation. Our physical health is dependent mostly on our living a healthy lifestyle and examining ourselves to look for signs of poor physical condition and illness. Self-examination is *also* essential for health and growth in the *spiritual* life of a Christian. This is because our *desperate need* is the only thing that will compel us to go to the Physician. If we do not desire spiritual health, or if we are not even aware of our illness, we will not be inclined to go to the doctor for treatment.

> Mark 2:17   And hearing this, Jesus said to them, "It is not those who are healthy who need a physician, but those who are sick; I did not come to call the righteous, but sinners."

We can see from the following verses how essential is *an accurate self-examination and diagnosis of one's own spiritual condition:*

> 2 Corinthians 13:5   Test yourselves to see if you are in the faith; examine yourselves! Or do you not recognize this about yourselves, that Jesus Christ is in you — unless indeed you fail the test?

> 1 Corinthians 11:28-32   But let a man examine himself, and so let him eat of the bread and drink of the cup. For he who eats and drinks, eats and drinks judgment to himself, if he does not judge the body rightly. For this reason many among you are weak and sick, and a number sleep. But if we judged ourselves rightly, we should not be judged. But when we are judged, we are disciplined by the Lord in order that we may not be condemned along with the world.

> Galatians 6:3-4   For if anyone thinks he is something when he is nothing, he deceives himself. But let each one examine his own work, and then he will have reason for boasting in regard to himself alone, and not in regard to another.

Further, the psalmist saw this evaluation as *requiring the aid of the Holy Spirit:*

> Psalm 139:23-24 Search me, O God, and know my heart; try me and know my anxious thoughts; and see if there be any hurtful way in me, and lead me in the everlasting way.

We need God's assistance in this for no other reason than that we are naturally sinful, full of self-deceit, and therefore cannot see our own faults clearly enough:

Jeremiah 17:9 "The heart is more deceitful than all else and is desperately sick; who can understand it?"

Psalm 19:12 Who can discern his errors? Acquit me of hidden faults.

This is very crucial to understand in the area of spiritual health. As in many physical diseases, a spiritual malady may be present before the symptoms become noticeable on the surface. This is why routine physical examinations are strongly recommended for even seemingly healthy people. This truth points to the spiritual reality that spiritual cancer can be hidden by a hypocritical profession of faith, or by an outward show of religion. Listen to the words of Jesus:

Matthew 15:8 "THIS PEOPLE HONORS ME WITH THEIR LIPS, BUT THEIR HEART IS FAR AWAY FROM ME."

The truth is, once again, that our heart is naturally bad, and in desperate need of the radical surgery of the spiritual "Cardiologist." And, the cancer of sin is a degenerative disease, which would cause our spiritual life to increasingly deteriorate, and eventually die, if it were not removed.

Believers must beware when they "feel well" and then gather confidence from this *seemingly* good condition that their spiritual state must therefore be favorable. Many believers expose themselves to spiritual ruin because they find encouragement in the lack of symptoms of spiritual disease. But, as the physical world reminds us, appearances can be deceiving! My sister-in-law was incredulous, considering how well she felt, and how physically healthy she appeared, when her physician informed her that she had leukemia. In her case the tests proved accurate regarding the disease, and she faced the most radical treatment in order to save her life. This picture from the physical world reflects the sad truth that spiritual disease may elude detection until it is too late.

Similarly, in the world of physical health, we may pretend that the symptoms of a serious disease are not really there, or we may mask the symptoms by pain-killing drugs that make us *feel* better *without treating the real cause of the pain.* Once again, this picture reflects the spiritual truth that many believers deceive themselves into thinking they are spiritually okay, or resort to superficial "remedies" that do little more than make them "feel better" and enjoy temporary relief from the pain. In this way, they avoid the radical treatment that is often necessary. For example, Jesus speaks of a spiritual treatment for lust that is as radical and painful as the physical amputation of a limb or the gouging out of an eyeball (Matthew 5:29-30). The treatment is absolutely necessary for continued spiritual life, but people often shrink from it, and chose instead to deceive themselves that they are "okay."

Finally, a physical disease like leprosy may destroy the physical senses, while it eats up the flesh, without the person even feeling it. A sad spiritual condition occurs where believers behave sinfully to their spiritual ruin, tearing their souls to pieces, and do not even feel the pain they bring on themselves.

Why is it so important that we engage in the painful task of self-examination and submitting to God's radical treatment *before* we can minister to our children? This thinking is the inevitable implication of the spiritual principle to which Jesus refers in Matthew 7. In order to be helpful spiritually to my brother (or my child!), I have to first have my spiritual "sight" restored by the removal of the sin which impedes my spiritual vision.

> Matthew 7:3-5 "And why do you look at the speck that is in your brother's eye, but do not notice the log that is in your own eye? Or how can you say to your brother, 'Let me take the speck out of your eye,' and behold, the log is in your own eye? You hypocrite, first take the log out of your own eye, and then you will see clearly to take the speck out of your brother's eye."

The principle of self-evaluation as applied to child rearing is that, if spiritual examination is necessary for the adult, it *is also necessary for the child.* The child has been entrusted to the oversight of the parent. God has wisely and kindly not left the child to himself to provide for his own spiritual health and well-being, any more than for his own physical health and well-being. What child would choose to go and get his shots or eat vegetables? *The parent has the major responsibility of seeing that the child's spiritual condition is evaluated and his infirmities treated effectively.*

TUESDAY

As we consider the practice of this principle, we will begin by asking ourselves a few questions about our *self*-examination. We cannot extend care to others for their spiritual needs if we have not already developed habits of taking care of our own needs. Are we in the practice of regularly judging ourselves spiritually (as we might examine our physical bodies for signs of illness) to discover our sins, in order to seek the Lord for His treatment? Have we, as parents, developed personal habits of self-evaluation? The Scriptures insist that the regular practice of this exercise is of life-and-death importance to our eternal well-being. What is our method in doing this in our own lives? Are we purposeful in this task of self-evaluation? Before we use the evaluation tools later for our children, therefore, we must first take the time to apply these tools to our own lives. And, we must resolve to develop a habit of self-examination for the future.

For now, we will expand our understanding of the importance of this practice of spiritual evaluation in our rearing of our children.

The importance of spiritual evaluation. Now is the time for forming the spiritual attitudes and habits and patterns in your child that will last a lifetime. Consider his special needs, his particular areas of sensitivity and vulnerability, his conspicuous faults or strengths which may become a snare if the Lord were not to intervene. Then set out to correct or improve them immediately. Consider the Scriptural teaching about the urgency of this practice:

Proverbs 22:6 Train up a child in the way he should go, even when he is old he will not depart from it.

This verse is often used for child training in the home. It has special reference to the correction and redirecting of a child with continuing effects for years to come. Actually, the verse is not so much an exhortation to training, as a *warning* that we need to "un-train." Bruce Ray bases his comments on a correct understanding of the original language:

> *...Proverbs 22:6 is not a promise so much as it is a warning* to Christian parents. In the *Hebrew* text of Proverbs 22:6, the phrase 'in the way he should go' is entirely lacking. Rather, the Hebrew says, 'Train up a child *in his way* and when he is old he will not depart from it.' Train up a child in *his* way or after *his* manner according to his ways. Allow a child to have self-expression, allow him to pick and to choose what he will and will not do, and as that habit is formed in his youth he will not change when he is older. If he does not learn discipline from you as a child he will never learn it as an adult. That is a warning.
>
> Bruce A. Ray, Withhold Not Correction
(Phillipsburg, NJ: Presbyterian & Reformed Pub. Co., 1978), p. 33

If we allow a child to confirm in his habits his own way, we leave him exposed to the danger and consequences of his ways. A general principle certainly applies to our children as well as to us adults:

Proverbs 14:12 There is a way which seems right to a man, but its end is the way of death.

To pursue the way that seems right according to our fallen wisdom leads to death. Although there are certainly implications here for *physical* life and death, the ultimate meaning concerns *spiritual* life and death. The meaning here is that if a man (or a child) follows the course of his sinful desires, without having his head and heart transformed to God's way, the consequence is eternal death.

These two passages (Proverbs 22:6 and 14:12), as they are taken together, present an ominous picture of the fate of a child who is left to pursue *his own* way. This is illustrated by the diagram to the right.

IN HIS OWN WAY

But the purpose of "child training" is to arrest the child's relentless pursuit of his own way, and redirect him toward the Lord and eternal happiness in Him. This is why evaluation is so important. So often, apart from Bible instruction, children are left alone (except when they *blatantly* sin). As we have seen, the Bible insists that *purposeful training* is necessary for the child to escape the natural course into which his sin nature takes him. We must not leave a child to his own way, or he will be hardened in his sinful path and never depart from it even to old age. The process of *redirecting the child*, therefore, as illustrated by the diagram on the next page, is the biblical remedy to the natural direction and destination of the sinners living in our home.

Once again, if this "*un-training*" does not happen, the child will be hardened in his way. And, the Scripture says that a person who has been set in his ways through childhood will continue in his way until death. Of course, the Lord can always apprehend the heart of a person who is bent on destruction, and graciously redirect him into the straight and narrow way. But the *natural* tendency of a hardened heart is to stay hard, and get harder still. The Scripture gives no encouragement for the good of a man who has not been "un-trained."

This principle applies to all areas of sin, and not just the "serious" sin. *All* sin is infection in the spiritual life, and if it is left untreated, it will become more and more serious. The smallest cancer cell, if given opportunity to multiply, will destroy the whole body. And, the longer sin is allowed to harden, the more difficult it will be to treat it successfully. Think about the relevance of what James says:

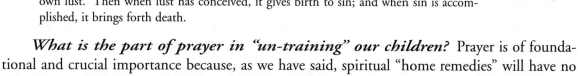

"UN-TRAIN"

> James 1:13-15 ...each one is tempted when he is carried away and enticed by his own lust. Then when lust has conceived, it gives birth to sin; and when sin is accomplished, it brings forth death.

What is the part of prayer in "un-training" our children? Prayer is of foundational and crucial importance because, as we have said, spiritual "home remedies" will have no effect on spiritual diseases. Prayer is taking our child to the Surgeon for His treatment.

At this point, we must bear in mind a common snare into which many Christian parents fall. It seems that a common attitude among parents is that to train a child means to *impose new behaviors on the child.* We tend to assume that, if we control and direct the behavior of our children, we have done our duty. We are therefore encouraged when we observe corrected behavior, and attribute the change to spiritual growth. This error is somewhat like a doctor giving a cancer patient a healthy diet and exercise program, while not removing the cancer. Although all physicians would no doubt agree that the patient's lifestyle is essential, none would say that a healthy lifestyle will be sufficient to cure a disease which has taken hold in a patient's body. Similarly, although we would all agree that godly behavior is essential for the Christian life, we should not assume that behavior change alone indicates spiritual health. It will not be helpful to add behavior patterns on the surface, while a child's deceptive desires remain untouched beneath. Prayer calls upon the Great Physician to cure the spiritual malady. Then, the corrected behavior will be due to a cured heart, rather than to outside restraints imposed on him.

Biblically, a person is not "trained" until he **prefers** *the godly behavior.* So often a child submits to his parents' principles and discipline as long as he lives under their roof. But, as soon as he "leaves the nest," his preferred behavior takes over. That is because his heart is still hard, and therefore when the restraints are removed, he shakes off the behavior and follows his own desires. Prayer calls upon God to do what HE must do, toward a new heart and life. ◯

Dear Stephanie,

   I think we tend to think of our dear children as neutral, and think that all we have to do is teach them. We kind of expect our children to choose the best way, and are confounded when our "Christian" children resist the Word! It's almost as though, when we teach them, we expect that they are just going to automatically embrace the good and reject the evil. Right? Wrong!

   Ward and June Cleaver never seemed to have this problem while raising Wally and "the Beav." Their sons, while they were mischievous ("boys will be boys"), were not really _evil_. Right? And, I think it was in the movie, _Boy's Town_, that Spencer Tracy said, "There's no such thing as a bad boy." Was he right?

   No. Sometimes we forget that there is an inbred hostility in our children to God and His ways. We underestimate the spiritual disease. Isn't it interesting that we didn't have to teach our (_even our!_) children to be selfish, and lie, hurt others, and be lazy and irresponsible? Even Christopher helps himself to the tortilla chips or cookies when we turn our backs, says "NO!" to our instructions, takes my watch, and hits his sister. They _all_ (even Christopher!) need a spiritual "heart transplant." Child rearing is like trying to renovate an old house. From the surface you see that it needs work. But when you remove the worn-out wood from the outside, you discover that the planks _underneath_ are rotten. You realize that more renovation is needed than you had assumed! And, if you put a fresh covering on top of the rotten wood, though it may look nice for awhile, it will collapse later. It's the same with child-rearing. If that old heart is not removed, everything that depends on it will eventually collapse.

   The encouragement here, as always, comes from the amazing love and forgiveness of our Father, and His power to change and save sinners from the inside out!

                                                    Love, Tim

Tim,

When I think about the need to "un-train" a child from his own natural ways, it really stings. I wish I had known ten years ago what I know now! There are so many <u>little</u> things that grow like acorns into very big trees, when it comes to undisciplined habits, aren't there? And you know better than anyone that it's <u>my own</u> areas of "challenge" that are the ones that flourish most in our children. Mary Poppins, I'm <u>not</u> ("practically perfect in every way")!

I think that one of the most difficult things as a parent is dealing with the "lowest common denominator" principle. If someone else's behavior isn't up to our stated standard, it becomes a challenge to us to change. For instance, we hear "So-and-so reads that series of books, and their family goes to church, so why can't <u>I</u> read them, too?" Or, "Friend A got to see that movie, so why won't you let <u>us</u> see it?" You know how often we have been betrayed by letting our guard down on such things, and the words, the pictures, the thought patterns are poured into those young minds before we realize it. Even the supposedly "safe" <u>old</u> movies have such awful role models of relationships between men and women, and formulas of <u>deception + humor = OK</u>.

These things bother me deeply, because it is in just such "inconsequential" recreational reading and entertainment that powerful images of ungodliness are slipped in "incognito." We aren't given a "delete" button on the top of their heads! How carefully we must take our role as guardians — according to Philippians 4:8, we and they must consider "whatever is true, whatever is noble, whatever is right, whatever is pure, whatever is lovely, whatever is admirable —if anything is excellent or praiseworthy," and "think about such things!"

When it comes to un-training, we have our work cut out for us, and we have no hope, but in the grace of God and His power, through the Word and prayer. May His grace be sufficient, even for me.

Love, Stephanie

WEDNESDAY

Our fourth child has Down Syndrome. We have learned that, if therapy is begun early in such a child's life, he will benefit greatly in his development. This is called "early intervention." If the treatment is delayed until a time past a certain age in the child's life, it will do little good for that child. This can be seen as a picture of the importance of beginning *spiritual* "therapy" early in life. It is indeed true that children in the depraved spiritual condition in which all children are born can develop to a point where spiritual training is much less effective. God can work at *any* time in a person's life to instill spiritual abilities. But, as far as it depends on us, we will benefit the most from training that is begun early. J. C. Ryle stresses the importance of training for a child's spiritual development, and highlights the consequences of the neglect of careful attention to a child's training *early in life*:

...Early habits (if I may so speak) are everything with us, under God. We are made what we are by training. Our character takes the form of that mold into which our first years are cast.

We depend, in a vast measure, on those who bring us up. We get from them a colour, a taste, a bias which cling to us more or less all our lives. We catch the language of our nurses and mothers, and learn to speak it almost insensibly, and unquestionably we catch something of their manners, ways, and mind at the same time. Time only will show, I suspect, how much we all owe to early impressions, and how many things in us may be traced up to seeds sown in the days of our very infancy, by those who were about us. A very learned Englishman, Mr. Locke, has gone so far as to say: 'That of all the men we meet with, nine parts out of ten are what they are, good or bad, useful or not, according to the education.'

And all this is one of God's merciful arrangements. He gives your children a mind that will receive impressions like moist clay. He gives them a disposition at the starting-point of life to believe what you tell them, and to take for granted what you advise them, and to trust your word rather than a stranger's. He gives you, in short, a golden opportunity of doing them good. See that the opportunity be not neglected, and thrown away. Once let slip, it is gone forever.

Beware of that miserable delusion into which some have fallen, — that parents can do nothing for their children, that you must leave them alone, wait for grace, and sit still....the devil rejoices to see such reasoning, just as he always does over anything which seems to excuse indolence, or to encourage neglect of means.

I know that you cannot convert your child. I know well that they who are born again are born, not of the will of man, but of God. But I know also that God says expressly, 'Train up a child in the way he should go,' and that He never laid a command on man which He would not give man grace to perform. And I know, too, that our duty is not to stand still and dispute, but to go forward and obey. It is just in the going forward that God will meet us. The path of obedience is the way in which He gives the blessing. We have only to do as the servants were commanded at the marriage feast in Cana, to fill the water-pots with water, and we may safely leave it to the Lord to turn that water into wine.

J. C. Ryle, *"Train Up A Child In The Way He Should Go" (The Duties of Parents)*, pp.6-8

Ryle stresses the importance of our part in shaping the character of our children. We are reminded of the various verses that stress the part we play in God's scheme of sovereign grace. For example, in 1 Corinthians 3, it is true that God gives the growth, but that does not make the planting and watering unnecessary.

1 Corinthians. 3:6 I planted, Apollos watered, but God was causing the growth.

Also, think of Philippians 2, which addresses our own sanctification, which is a matter of working out what God has already worked in. The work that God has done in us does not negate the place of our subsequent work, which is founded on His work.

Philippians 2:12-13 So then, my beloved, just as you have always obeyed, not as in my presence only, but now much more in my absence, work out your salvation with fear and trembling; for it is God who is at work in you, both to will and to work for His good pleasure.

Regarding the work of "un-training" our children, *we need to constantly be reminded of how naturally our sinful habits come to us, and how easily we are infected by the patterns of the world around us.* As Francis Schaeffer used to say, we catch world views much the same as we catch colds. *It's the same way with our habitual behaviors and attitudes.* Our sin natures are spring-loaded to respond to sinful patterns, and such patterns, once they take hold, are hard to cure.

And, if you allow *even one sin* to remain unchecked and uncorrected, if it continues, it could spell your child's later spiritual downfall. At best, unchecked sin in one's life can lead to untold misery in life and ineffectiveness in a Christian's service. As Jonathan Edwards says, sins not dealt with in younger life get stronger in later life:

I observe that old men seldom have any advantage of new discoveries, because they are beside the way of thinking to which they have been so long used. Resolved, if ever I live to years, that I will be impartial to hear the reasons of all pretended discoveries, and receive them if rational, how long soever I have been used to another way of thinking....

I observe that there are some evil habits, which do increase and grow stronger, even in some good people, as they grow older; habits that much obscure the beauty of Christianity: some things which are according to their natural tempers, which in some measure prevail when they are young in Christ, and the evil disposition having an unobserved control, the habit at last grows very strong, and commonly regulates the practice until death. By this means, old Christians are very commonly, in some respects, more unreasonable than those who are young.

Jonathan Edwards, *Works*, vol. One, p. xxxi, xxxv

Edwards, in a sermon on Hosea 5:15, also warns of the tendency of our fallen human nature to be hardened over time, as people resist the convictions God places in their hearts regarding their sins:

Their hearts now are become harder for light, and convictions being once conquered, they evermore are an occasion of a greater hardness of heart than they were before. Yea, there is no one thing whatsoever, which has so great a tendency to it. Man's heart is hardened by losing convictions, as iron is hardened by being heated and cooled. If you are awakened, and afterwards lose your convictions, it will be a harder thing to awaken you again. If there were only that you are growing older, there would be less probability of your being awakened again; for as persons grow older they grow less and less susceptible of convictions; evil habits grow stronger and more deeply rooted in the heart. You greatly offend God by quenching his Spirit, and returning as a dog to his vomit, and as a sow that was washed to her wallowing in the mire.

Jonathan Edwards, *Works*, vol. Two, p. 837

Let us as parents, if we love our children, not allow them to confirm their sinful ways toward disaster in their lives, but let us be very purposeful in "un-training" them of their folly, and replacing it with the divine ways and patterns that lead in the way everlasting (Psalm 139:24).

And, let us not make the mistake of thinking we can put this vital parental responsibility off until a later time. Consider very seriously the dire warning of Proverbs 27, which reminds us that, for all we know, we may not have any tomorrows:

Proverbs 27:1   Do not boast about tomorrow, for you do not know what a day may bring forth.

THURSDAY

How do we train them (or, "un-train" them)? The first step, of course, is to *find out their sinful ways.* That is the reason the Spiritual Evaluation is so important. In the evaluation process, we will take the child to the Lord, Who is the *Great Physician*, in order to evaluate his spiritual health, and then put together a scriptural "health regimen" for the child's recovery of spiritual life and health. Also, we will lay the foundation for a continued healthy spiritual lifestyle, as well as identify areas of life which require treatment and therapy at the present time.

THE FOLLOWING TWO TOOLS ARE RECOMMENDED TO ASSIST PARENTS IN THE SPIRITUAL EVALUATION OF THEIR CHILDREN:

1) The SPIRITUAL INVENTORY WORKSHEET is the first tool designed for assisting parents in this spiritual evaluation. The worksheet is located after Saturday's study (on pages 106-107).

-In using this sheet, first pray that the Lord will help you to see and think clearly about your child, so that you will not miss or misread vital facts.

-It is helpful to think of the picture of the doctor assessing a child's condition, while taking careful note of the pitfalls and dangers of evaluating your own child. The wise words of H. Clay Trumbull are very instructive:

No quality of a good physician is of more importance than skill in making a diagnosis of a patient's case....until the diagnosis is accurate, the best efforts of the ablest physician are liable to be misdirected, and so to be ineffective for good. As it is with the physician and his patient, so it is with the parent and his child. An accurate diagnosis is an essential prerequisite to wise and efficient treatment. The diagnosis secured, the matter of treatment is a comparatively easy matter. A parent's diagnosis of his child's case is in the discerning of his child's faults, as preliminary to a process of train-

ing for their cure. Until that is secured, there is no hope of intelligent and well-direct ed treatment.

Yet it is not the easiest thing in the world to say what are a child's peculiar faults, and what is, therefore, that child's peculiar need of training. Many a parent is disturbed by a child's best traits, while he underestimates or overlooks the child's chief failings.... "That boy's questions will worry my life out. He is always asking questions; and such questions. I can't stand it!" This is said by many a father or mother whose child is full of promise, largely because he is full of questions.

But if a boy has a bright mind and positive preferences, and is ready to study or to work untiringly in the line of his own tastes, and in no other line, it does not always occur to his parents that just here — in this reluctance to apply himself in the line of wise expediency rather than of personal fancy — there is a failing which, if not trained out of that boy, will stand as a barrier to his truest manhood....

Careful study and a wise discrimination are needed on a parent's part to ascertain a child's peculiar faults. Each parent would do well to ask himself, or herself, the questions, "What are the special faults of my child? Where is he weakest? In what direction is his greatest strength liable to lead him astray, and when is it most likely to fail him? Which of his faults is most prominent? Which of them is of chief importance for immediate correction?"

H. Clay Trumbull, *Hints on Child Training*, pp. 14-15

- We will fill out a SPIRITUAL INVENTORY WORKSHEET *for each child, being as specific as possible.* We will fill this out on Saturday. The instructions are on page 103.

-Having identified the areas of need in your child, design a treatment plan appropriate for that child. This should include prayer that the Lord will change his heart, as well as a discipline procedure to change the behavior. Make sure you do not avoid including or administering treatment on the grounds that it would be painful for the child. You would not want your physician to exclude needed treatment of his physical problems because such treatment would be unpleasant. Consider:

Hebrews 12:5-11 And you have forgotten the exhortation which is addressed to you as sons, MY SON, DO NOT REGARD LIGHTLY THE DISCIPLINE OF THE LORD, NOR FAINT WHEN YOU ARE REPROVED BY HIM; FOR THOSE WHOM THE LORD LOVES HE DISCIPLINES, AND HE SCOURGES EVERY SON WHOM HE RECEIVES."

It is for discipline that you endure; God deals with you as with sons; for what son is there whom his father does not discipline? But if you are without discipline, of which all have become partakers, then you are illegitimate children and not sons. Furthermore, we had earthly fathers to discipline us, and we respected them; shall we not much rather be subject to the Father of spirits, and live? For they disciplined us for a short time as seemed best to them, but He disciplines us for our good, that we may share His holiness. All discipline for the moment seems not to be joyful, but sorrowful; yet to those who have been trained by it, afterwards it yields the peaceful fruit of righteousness.

Proverbs 13:24 He who spares his rod hates his son, but he who loves him disciplines him diligently.

Proverbs 22:15 Foolishness is bound up in the heart of a child; the rod of discipline will remove it far from him.

Proverbs 23:13-14 Do not hold back discipline from the child.
  Although you beat him with the rod, he will not die.
You shall beat him with the rod, and deliver his soul from Sheol.

FRIDAY

In going through the evaluation process, it is also wise to seek the counsel of trusted and competent "outsiders," or any objective observer of your child, to assist you in this all-important task of the evaluation and diagnosis of your child. Of course, there is a sense in which you are yourself in a unique position to know your child, since you live with him and probably have known him since infancy. But it is also true that your personal closeness to your child may lead you to overlook or ignore vital factors, which may result in a biased conclusion.

In a task which is so vital, do not neglect the counsel of the Body of Christ, and others, and its value in assisting you in knowing and helping your child toward spiritual health and life. Consider the words of H. Clay Trumbull:

> The unfriendly criticisms of neighbors, and the kind suggestions of friends, are not to be despised by a parent in making up an estimate of his child's failings and faults. Rarely is a parent so discerning, so impartial, and so wise, that he can know his children through and through, and be able to weigh the several traits, and perceive the every imperfection and exaggeration, of their characters, with unerring accuracy and absolute fairness. A judge is supposed to be disqualified for an impartial hearing of a case in which he has a direct personal interest. A physician will not commonly make a diagnosis of his own disorders, lest his fears or hopes should bias his judgment. And a parent is as liable as a judge or a physician to be swayed unduly by interest or affection, in an estimate of a case which is before him for a decision....
>
> If a parent were explicitly to ask the question of a fair and plain-speaking friend, familiar with that parent's children, and competent to judge them, 'What do you think is the chief fault — or the most objectionable characteristic — of my son — or daughter?' the frank answer to that question would in very many cases be an utter surprise to the parent, the fault or characteristic named not having been suspected by the parent. A child may be so much like the parent here, that the parent's blindness to his or her own chief fault or lack may forbid the seeing of the child's similar deformity. Or, again, that child may be so totally unlike the parent, that the parent will be unable to appreciate, or even to apprehend, that peculiarity of the child which is apparent to every outside intelligent observer....
>
> Parents need help from others, from personal friends whom they can trust to speak with impartiality and kindness, or from the teachers of their children, in the gaining of a proper estimate and understanding of their children's characteristics and needs. The parent who does not realize this truth, and act on it, will never do as well as might be done for his or her child. God has given the responsibility of the training of that child to the parent; but He has also laid on that parent the duty of learning, by the aid of all proper means, what are the child's requirements, and how to meet them.
>
> H. Clay Trumbull, *Hints on Child Training*, pp. 15-17

We can also benefit from the sobering reminder of J. C. Ryle concerning the sad limitations imposed by our sinful nature on our powers of observation in the case of our own children:

> ...men can see the faults of their neighbors more clearly than their own. They will often bring up their children in the very path which they have denounced to their friends as unsafe. They will see motes in other men's families, and overlook beams in their own. They will be quicksighted as eagles in detecting mistakes abroad, and yet blind as bats to fatal errors which are daily going on at

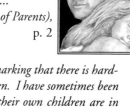

home. They will be wise about their brother's house, but foolish about their own flesh and blood. Here, if anywhere, we have need to suspect our own judgment....

J. C. Ryle, *"Train Up A Child In The Way He Should Go" (The Duties of Parents),*
p. 2

[In a footnote, on the same page, Ryle writes: *"As a minister, I cannot help remarking that there is hardly any subject about which people seem so tenacious as they are about their children. I have sometimes been perfectly astonished at the slowness of sensible Christian parents to allow that their own children are in fault, or deserve blame. There are not a few persons to whom I would far rather speak about their own sins, than tell them their children had done anything wrong."*]

SATURDAY

2) The second tool that we will offer for spiritual evaluation is the SPIRITUAL PROGRESS EVALUATION WORKSHEET. This sheet, the use of which will be introduced in detail next Monday, is designed for the evaluation of a person's progress (whether he be an adult or a child!) in pursuing *personal godliness*. The SPIRITUAL PROGRESS EVALUATION WORKSHEET identifies forty-five aspects of the life of faith, and helps us to consider the degree to which a person has attained spiritual progress in each area.

This worksheet provides a structure for use in working through the various areas of the Christian life and relationships in a *regular and systematic way*. It also provides a structure for *charting progress* toward greater and greater likeness to Jesus. Over a number of weeks (it is recommended that a week be devoted to each area), the person's mastery of the different areas of godliness will be monitored, and progress will be sought.

It sets out to build a strong biblical foundation for life, in that it focuses on mastering the teachings of Scripture. Then it proceeds toward implanting the teaching in life for producing a harvest of righteousness for the Lord. This tool is based on the understanding that our whole life in this world is to be a training ground for eternal life with God. It sees the importance of seizing every opportunity and resource that God gives us, and purposefully making it the servant of the goal of moving toward Him and greater fellowship with Him. After all, it is *God*, and fellowship with *Him*, that makes heaven *really* heaven for the Christian (see Psalm 73:25).

Before we set out on the business of "self-examination," we need to make a very important point in order to clarify our grasp of the place of self-examination in the Christian life. This point has to do with our desire that our children experience the "assurance of salvation." How can they be confident that they actually possess eternal life? Often people are told that they can be certain of their salvation on the basis of their believing the Gospel truth that Christ died for them, and of their reciting a particular prayer to God for their salvation. While it is true that belief in the Gospel and calling out to God are necessary to receive salvation, our *dying to sin* and *godly life* are the keys to our assurance that we truly belong to God. Listen to Peter's words:

2 Peter 1:5-11 For this very reason, make every effort to add to your faith goodness; and to goodness, knowledge; and to knowledge, self-control; and to self-control, perseverance; and to perseverance, godliness; and to godliness, brotherly kindness; and to brotherly kindness, love. For if you possess these qualities in increasing measure, they will keep you from being ineffective and unproductive in your knowledge of our Lord Jesus Christ. But if anyone does not have them, he is nearsighted and blind, and has forgotten that he has been cleansed from his past sins. Therefore, my brothers, be all the more eager to make your calling and election sure. For if you do these things, you will never fall, and you will receive a rich welcome into the eternal kingdom of our Lord and Savior Jesus Christ. (NIV)

Jonathan Edwards and Henry Scougal express this extremely significant biblical thinking:

It is not God's design that men should obtain assurance in any other way, than by mortifying corruption, and increasing in grace, and obtaining the lively exercises of it. — And although self-examination be a duty of great use and importance, and by no means to be neglected; yet it is not the *principal* means, by which the saints do get satisfaction of their good estate. Assurance is not to be obtained so much by *self-examination*, as by *action*. The Apostle Paul sought assurance chiefly this way, even by *forgetting the things that were behind, and reaching forth unto those things that were before, pressing towards the mark for the prize of the high calling of God in Christ Jesus; if by any means he might attain unto the resurrection of the dead.* And it was by this means chiefly that he obtained assurance: 1 Cor. 9:26, "I therefore so run, not as uncertainly." He obtained assurance of winning the prize, more by *running*, than by *considering.* The *swiftness of his pace* did more towards his assurance of a conquest, than the *strictness of his examination.* Giving all diligence to grow in grace, by adding to faith, virtue, &c., is the direction that the Apostle Peter gives us, for *making our calling and election sure*, and having *an entrance ministered to us abundantly, into Christ's everlasting kingdom.* Without this, our eyes will be dim, and we shall be as men in the dark; we cannot plainly see either the forgiveness of our sins past, or our heavenly inheritance that is future, and *far off,* 2 Pet. 1:5-11.

Jonathan Edwards, *Works,* vol. One, p. 263

These [speaking of the four graces of *love for God, charity for men, purity* and *humility*] are the highest perfections that either men or angels are capable of; the very foundation of heaven laid in the soul; and he who hath attained them need not desire to pry into the hidden rolls of God's decrees, or search the volumes of heaven to know what is determined about his everlasting condition; but he may find a copy of God's thoughts concerning him written in his own breast. His love to God may give him assurance of God's favor to him; and those beginnings of happiness which he feels in the conformity of the powers of his soul to the nature of God, and compliance with his will, are a sure pledge that his felicity shall be perfected and continued to all eternity; and it is not without reason that one said: "I had rather see the real impressions of a godlike nature upon my own soul, than to have a vision from heaven, or angel sent to tell me that my name were enrolled in the book of life."

Henry Scougal, *The Life of God in the Soul of Man,* pp. 48-49

The design of these evaluation worksheets is based on this biblical thinking. We desire that our children be truly saved, and that their assurance of this reality rest on their *actually possessing in increasing measure that spiritual life and health that is indeed of God.* That is why we devote so much time and effort to this eternally important task.

Today, in concluding this week, and before we get to the SPIRITUAL PROGRESS EVALUATION WORKSHEET next week, we will look at the first of these tools, the SPIRITUAL INVENTORY WORKSHEET. We will prayerfully begin filling out copies of the sheet for each disciple (including one adapted for use by yourself). *Keep in mind the words of explanation for this worksheet that we covered during Thursday's and Friday's teaching times.*

We will now briefly look at the specific questions that comprise the SPIRITUAL INVENTORY WORKSHEET. As we consider the questions, you can refer to the worksheet on pages 106-107.

First, it will be relatively easy, though important, to identify your child's *good* points. What are the talents and abilities that shine in your child? In what areas can you truly and honestly affirm and encourage him? What aspects of his personality have potential for developing into something special?

Once you have identified some positive areas, think about how these strengths and traits have potential to benefit the child in *spiritual pursuits*. It may be somewhat easier to think of worldly pursuits for which your child's gifts particularly equip him. But do not overlook the more important pursuit in your child's life, the pursuit of God. In this, we are basing our thinking on the fact that our child's *chief end* is to *glorify God and enjoy Him forever* (Westminster Shorter Catechism). This means that everything God has given to your child, whether it be resources or gifts or abilities, should be devoted to the goal of knowing and pleasing and loving and enjoying God. It would be tragic indeed to see those precious characteristics and abilities wasted on selfish or worldly pursuits. Set out to assist your child in striving to invest his assets in heavenly pursuits.

Also, however, think carefully about how these positive traits may become snares for your child, and possibly fail him or lead him astray. In what ways could his strengths actually become his downfall?

Second, consider your child's *passions*. What are the things that make his eyes light up? What are his interests? What does he love to do in life? Then, think about how these passions can be redirected so that they may give way to superior spiritual enjoyment. Remember, we are very vulnerable to idolatry, to looking to the pleasures of this world for happiness instead of God Himself. What things might become your child's gods if God does not intervene? Identify things in this world that may distract your child from God, or might choke out the Word (Mark 4:18-19) when it is "sown."

Third, observe your child's *particular faults and chief failings*. Identifying your child's faults and failings is a delicate task indeed, simply because your child will likely possess some of *your own* faults and failings! Think soberly and prayerfully about this, and consider very carefully the counsel of other people.

Fourth, it is crucial that we identify our child's *weaknesses and vulnerabilities*. This is crucial because these are the places where Satan will launch his attack on your child's soul. He knows where your child is weak and vulnerable, so special prayer is needed for God's protection in those areas.

Fifth, give attention also to your child's *temperamental or emotional weaknesses* that may impede his growth toward God.

Sixth, and finally, determine from this inventory what specific areas in your child's life and situation require *prayer*. This will then be the reference point on your daily prayer list (#8). ◇

[**NOTE**: For an explanation of the CLOUD and ARROW GRAPHIC, see the introduction to the other worksheet next Monday.]

Dear Stephanie,

What makes our children's eyes light up? What "pulls their chain"? What is exciting to them? Steph, isn't it fun to watch our children get so elated about their childhood interests? I envy that zest for life!

We want our children to have a growing passion for the Lord. What do we do with our children's _other_ passions? Squelch them? No. Childhood passions like playing, doggies, Star Wars, Indians, toy guns, American Girls, Beanie Babies, model cars, and junk food naturally give rise to "adult" passions like sports, career, sex, cars, movies, vacations, money, and junk food. In the natural course of growing up, people just transfer their passions from childhood toys to grown-up toys. And, it is said, "He who dies with the most toys wins."

How many "grown up" _Christians_ never outgrow their passions for the things of this world? They believe in Him, but _really_ are more passionate about the enjoyments, and rewards, and honors, of this life. How many do not see their passions of this life _give way_ to _spiritual_ passions? How many never seem to wake up to the fact that none of the toys of this world can satisfy for long? And, when "the novelty wears off," the tragic thing is that people seem so rarely to turn from the vain passions of this world to set their hearts on "things above" (Col. 3:1-3).

Paul's all-consuming passion was Christ. He says, "I consider everything a loss compared to the surpassing greatness of knowing Christ Jesus my Lord, for whose sake I have lost all things. I consider them rubbish, that I may gain Christ" (Phil. 3:8, NIV).

Nobody has to tell a young adult, "Now, quit having fun, doing childhood things. Now it's time to do 'grown-up' things." No. They lose interest in childhood toys. May that be true spiritually, as well.

Let's really pray that our children would "grow up" early: that their passions would grow into _true passion_ for _God_. Revival in the church won't happen until our children are passionate, but not about sports, or food, or hobbies, or vacations, or politics, or entertainment, but rather passionate for _Christ_. An _all-consuming_ passion is what we need to pray for!

Love, Tim

A Note from Stephanie...

Tim,

    I am reminded of how Keith has always had an interest in toy weapons, pretending to be an Indian, with his bow and arrow, or Robin Hood with his flashing sword! Now that he is getting older, his joy in these plastic arrows and swords has given way to an interest in _real_ archery, and the _real_ swords on display in flea markets, etc..

    Melissa, too, who has always loved her dolls, is growing more and more interested in _real_ babies. And, I am so glad to note, the desire to make "food" out of play-doh is giving way to the requests to "let me cook" with _real_ food on its way to our dining room table!

    These are the things that picture for me what you are talking about in terms of having our passions transferred to higher, more spiritual passions. No one is telling Keith, "You can't play with your pink and green plastic sword anymore." He has simply matured in his interests. Melissa can still make a fine plate of play-doh cookies, but she'd _rather_ use oatmeal and chocolate chips.

    Let us strive to pray for and otherwise nurture a love for the deeper, richer experiences of life with Christ — that ministering to others and bringing glory to His Name might become their passion — a passion that they might "catch" from us!

Love, Stephanie

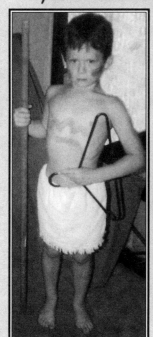

SPIRITUAL INVENTORY WORKSHEET

NAME: _____ **AGE:** _____ **DATE:** _____

1. What are this child's greatest strengths and best traits, and in what ways do these have potential for spiritual good in his life? In what ways are these traits most likely to fail him or lead him astray?

```



PICTURE



```

2. What are this child's passions? How might they be redirected toward spiritual pursuits? From what worldly pleasures or treasures does he need to be weaned, to avoid their becoming his gods?

3. What are this child's particular faults and chief failings, and which are most prominent and in need of immediate correction? Which faults or failings, if not corrected, could lead to shipwreck of his faith?

4. In which areas is he spiritually vulnerable? What are his fears? Is he particularly sensitive in some ways?

5. What are temperamental or emotional weaknesses that could impede his spiritual growth?

6. From the above inventory, in what specific spiritual areas is this child in particular need of prayer?

A Note from Stephanie...

Tim,

I am so glad to have these inventory and evaluation forms — something <u>concrete</u> to help focus and direct my prayers for each child. So often I have had a general sense of strength or weakness in them regarding one or another aspect of their characters, but it is <u>so</u> useful to take the time to stop and look at the Scriptures as the measure to "diagnose" where we stand. They say, "If you aim at nothing, you're sure to hit it," but I want to have real, personal goals to pray for, so we will move toward progress and growth in God's eyes. If they are to be transformed into the image of Christ, we need to know what raw material we're asking Him to work with!

It will be satisfying, I believe, to go through these sheets again some months down the road and see how God has worked in various facets of each child's life. That He would choose to use my prayers as an artist's tools in the sculpting of these "earthen vessels" is very humbling indeed. And to be convicted that we have not because we ask not (James 4:2), gives me even greater motivation to more accurately identify needs for prayer!

Because convictions do have a "shelf life" (meaning that if we don't act on them, they grow weak and ineffective), I know I will need to read through the first part of this book at least once more this year, and perhaps every January after that. Let's plan on going over these sheets together every New Year and every summer (perhaps just before or after our anniversary), OK? We won't want to miss the opportunities to observe the fruit of His work in each child in response to our prayers and weekly Scripture studies, will we? I am looking forward to many more joys ahead!

Love, Stephanie

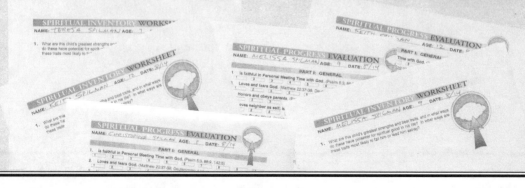

Dear Stephanie,

"Why take all this time and effort to evaluate?" Some parents may think we might be taking this too seriously: "After all, every kid needs the same thing: salvation! Why do we need this evaluation? Let's just pray! Time's a-wastin'!"

It's right that we need to pray without delay. But the time and effort that we devote to this evaluation will help us make that prayer more effective. If Christopher Robin were to pray for his friends, Pooh Bear would have different needs than Owl, and Piglet different needs than Eeyore. Think about Dennis the Menace: wouldn't his parents emphasize different things in their prayer for him than Margaret's parents do for her? Do Charlie Brown's parents need to pray as much for his prideful nature as Lucy's parents do? Then, what are the _particular_ needs of these various children? Since each child is different than the next, we need to pray differently in some sense for each child.

The profound differences between children will determine the areas we _emphasize_ in prayer. It's true that all children are sinners, but the _form_ that sin takes is often affected by the child's personality, temperament, experiences, etc. All people need the medical attention of their physician, but not all have the same specific diseases or health needs. Since Christopher has Down Syndrome, his needs can be much different than Keith's. Since one of our nieces has diabetes, her health needs will be different than her sister's or brother's, who don't have that disease. It's the same with spiritual needs. But few parents try to determine the specific _spiritual_ health needs of each of their children.

It has been a challenging task, "evaluating" our children, hasn't it? But I really have been amazed with how much more focused and purposeful my prayer has been for them.

Love, Tim

Personal Meeting Time:

THE WORD

The Word Preached / Taught

Scripture Reading

Personal Reading / Study

SUNDAY

Sermon / teaching:

Scripture reading:

Personal reading / study:

Items for Prayer

MONDAY

Scripture reading: Mark 2:17; 2 Cor 13:5; 1 Cor 11:28-32; Gal 6:3-4; Psalm 139:23-24; Jer 17:9; Psalm 19:12; Matt 15:8

Personal reading / study:

Items for Prayer

TUESDAY

Scripture reading: Proverbs 22:6; Proverbs 14:12; James 1:13-15

Personal reading / study:

Items for Prayer

WEDNESDAY

Scripture reading: 1 Corinthians 3:6; Philippians 2:12-13; Psalm 139:24; Proverbs 27:1

Personal reading / study:

Items for Prayer

THURSDAY

Scripture reading: Hebrews 12:5-11; Proverbs 13:24, 22:15, 23:13-14

Personal reading / study:

Items for Prayer

FRIDAY

Scripture reading: Meditate on the passages we have already used this week

Personal reading / study:

Items for Prayer

SATURDAY

Scripture reading: 2 Peter 1:1-11

Personal reading / study:

Items for Prayer

WEEK 4 - SUMMARY SHEET
GUIDING QUESTIONS

[**NOTE:** *These questions, which are to be answered in the spaces below, are to guide you in reflecting on each day's content.* **All** *of the questions will not be answered* **every** *day, but only those that are helpful in processing a particular day's material.*]

1. In what specific ways has my thinking and practice been challenged or transformed by my interaction with today's biblical teaching? What particular teaching will require further study and reflection?

2. For what specific wrong thinking, sinful priorities, or areas of neglect in my responsibility, must I make confession and seek the forgiveness of the Lord?

3. Seeing that I am now responsible to strive to make the Word I have received today a reality in my life, what specifically must I do in response to God? How specifically will my life and relationships be different as a result of my time with God today? What vows might I make to the Lord this Sunday regarding my intentions to be faithful to Him in particular areas? And, seeing that, in order for this life change to become a reality, God must powerfully work by His grace and through His Spirit in my life, what specifically must I ask God to do or provide?

4. Upon what particular Bible verses will I meditate throughout the day? What verses do I desire to post in a conspicuous place to remind me to meditate upon them? What verses will I commit to memory?

MONDAY

TUESDAY

WEDNESDAY

THURSDAY

FRIDAY

SATURDAY

SPIRITUAL EVALUATION

EXPLANATION

As we saw last week, the SPIRITUAL PROGRESS EVALUATION WORKSHEET is a tool designed to assist Christians in the ongoing discipleship task of pursuing *personal godliness*. This week we will look at this sheet and begin using it in our discipleship. The sheet is at the end of this week's studies.

MONDAY

The graphic we will use (see *below left*) consists of an arrow and a cloud. The arrow, which stands for our upward progress, is pointing toward a picture of a cloud, which stands for God. The cloud is a symbol that God used many times in Old Testament times to indicate His presence and power among His people.

As we have seen before, the cloud is *not a picture of God*. Rather, it shows the hiddenness of the divine nature, the mysteriousness of His essence, and the fact that He is above and beyond creation. God Himself is *beyond* the cloud; He is separate from all creation.

The circle around the cloud picture is like a window which reminds us that, though God exists in a different and separate "dimension," He is nevertheless accessible to us through the Word and prayer. We can "see" the spiritual world beyond the window through the "eyes" of faith, through the Word. The cloud, though, reminds us that our "sight" is still limited by our sinful human nature in this world. Our goal in the Christian life is to move toward God in everything (thus, the arrow). The progress that we make through the character traits on the SPIRITUAL PROGRESS EVALUATION WORKSHEET means *progress toward God and fellowship with Him*. After all, our "chief end," according to the old catechism, is to "glorify God and to enjoy Him forever." And, as one pastor/theologian (John Piper) put it, "God is most glorified in us when we are most satisfied in Him." What does it mean to be satisfied in Him? Jesus said,

John 14:21 "Whoever has my commands and obeys them, he is the one who loves me. He who loves me will be loved by my Father, and I too will love him and show myself to him." (NIV)

Jesus says later, in a prayer to the Father on behalf of believers:

John 17:24   "Father, I desire that they also, whom Thou hast given Me, be with Me where I am, in order that they may behold My glory, which Thou hast given Me; for Thou didst love Me before the foundation of the world."

The whole goal of obedience is that God, Who is pleased when we look to Him in faith in His grace for our holiness and progress in godliness, will grant us more and more of a spiritual sight of His glory in Christ. In "seeing" and enjoying and being more and more satisfied in all that He is for us, we are blessed. We look to God, and the enjoyment of Him, for happiness. This is the goal of life, and the goal of spiritual progress. As we embark on this spiritual venture, let us be reminded by the picture of the arrow and the cloud that *God Himself*, and *the enjoyment of Him*, is our *ultimate goal!*

And the spiritual principle is that the more we progress toward God, the more vigorous will be our striving toward Him. The more we have of Him, the more we will want of Him. Meditate on the following words of Jonathan Edwards from his profound book, *The Religious Affections*:

> The more a true saint loves God with a gracious love, the more he desires to love him, and the more uneasy is he at his want [lack] of love to him; the more he hates sin, the more he desires to hate it, and laments that he has so much remaining love to it; the more he mourns for sin, the more he longs to mourn for sin; the more his heart is broken, the more he desires it should be broken; the more he thirsts and longs after God and holiness, the more he longs to long, and breathe out his very soul in longings after God: the kindling and raising of gracious affections is like kindling a flame; the higher it is raised, the more ardent it is; and the more it burns, the more vehemently does it tend and seek to burn. So that the spiritual appetite after holiness, and an increase of holy affections is much more lively and keen in those that are eminent in holiness, than others, and more when grace and holy affections are in their most lively exercise, than at other times. It is as much the nature of one that is spiritually new born, to thirst after growth in holiness, as it is the nature of a new born babe to thirst after the mother's breast; who has the sharpest appetite, when best in health. 1 Pet. 2:2, 3, "As new born babes, desire the sincere milk of the word, that ye may grow thereby: if so be ye have tasted that the Lord is gracious." The most that the saints have in this world, is but a taste, a prelibation of that future glory which is their proper fullness; it is only an earnest of their future inheritance in their hearts, 2 Cor. 1:22, and 5:5, and Eph. 1:14. The most eminent saints in this state are but children, compared with their future, which is their proper state of maturity and perfection; as the apostle observes, 1 Cor. 13:10, 11. The greatest eminency that the saints arrive to in this world, has no tendency to satiety, or to abate their desires after more; but, on the contrary, makes them more eager to press forwards; as is evident by the apostle's words, Phil. 3:13, 14, 15: "Forgetting those things which are behind, and reaching forth unto those things which are before, I press towards the mark. — Let us therefore, as many as be *perfect*, be thus minded."
>
> Jonathan Edwards, *Works*, vol. One, p. 312

Our desire then, is that this work will be begun and flourish in our children as we progress. As we said before, we are not after mere behavior change, but transformed affections. We are after a life that reflects a true love for God and desires for Him.

Having considered these very important points today, we will continue tomorrow our explanation of the SPIRITUAL PROGRESS EVALUATION WORKSHEET. ◇

Today we will summarize the *objective*, the *design*, and the *plan* of the SPIR-ITUAL PROGRESS EVALUATION WORKSHEET. *Refer to the worksheet that follows this week's study.*

1. Objective.

This "system" has a three-part objective:

TUESDAY

a. To facilitate the mastering of the teaching of the Word of God concerning each of the areas on the SPIRITUAL PROGRESS EVALUATION WORKSHEET;

b. To assist the disciple and the discipler in identifying areas of life which are in need of grace and improvement (that is, in need of *prayer* and *hard work*); and

c. To provide a framework for evaluating progress in our striving toward improvement in grace in each of the areas of life.

2. Design.

This tool is designed for use by individual Christians in the task of discipleship, or by families with children. This spiritual progress method can be used as a tool in general discipleship for Christians, whether by an individual person in his own spiritual life, or by an established Christian in discipling a new believer. It can be especially helpful to any and every Christian who has not developed a regular discipline of evaluating his spiritual life, and keeping track of his personal spiritual progress.

It has a special use, though, in assisting parents in discipling their own children in conjunction with the PRAYER FOR MY CHILD guide. It should first be used by both Christian parents in their own lives, and then implemented in each of their children's lives.

The design has two elements:

a. The SPIRITUAL PROGRESS EVALUATION WORKSHEET. On this worksheet, we have identified forty-five areas in life, and have provided the Scriptural foundation upon which to build in each one. The design of this worksheet has three parts. We begin in **Part I** with general aspects of the healthy life of faith (love for and dependence on God, loving others, purity, humility, and service); then we move to **Part II**, heart and behavior characteristics (the fruit of the Spirit); and end up, in **Part III**, in the practical outworking of the first two categories (relationships and responsibilities). The following approach is recommended as a procedure for using the SPIRITUAL PROGRESS EVALUATION WORKSHEET:

1) Conduct an INITIAL EVALUATION of the person in each of the forty-five areas. The first step is to fill out the evaluation. Under each character area is a series of boxes labeled from 1 to 10. The task is to evaluate the present degree of

conformity or faithfulness or obedience to the Word in each area. The box labeled "**1**" indicates the most minimal conformity or obedience to the Word in that area, "**10**" means the greatest conformity or obedience, and the varying degrees of more or less conformity or obedience are indicated by the boxes in between. In each of the 45 areas, mark with a red or yellow colored pencil or highlighting marker the box that seems closest to the person's present attainment in that area. **NOTE**: You will no doubt find that there are a number of areas in which you do not have a basis for evaluation from observation of that character trait in the person to *any* degree. This should be a powerful clue to you that NO PURPOSEFUL WORK has been attempted in putting these particular Scripture teachings into practice in his life. Let that motivate you to begin the work and prayer needed in these areas, so that an evaluation of *tangible evidence of grace* in these aspects of godliness can be attained in the next evaluation. As you can see, no possible evaluation is an evaluation nonetheless, an evaluation that reveals a lack of godliness in a particular area.

2) REPEAT THE EVALUATION after a period of time. The SPIRITUAL PROGRESS EVALUATION WORKSHEET will be filled out again on the person in six months or so (giving special attention at that time to the particular traits focused on during the time since the last evaluation), and yet another evaluation should be conducted about six months after that. A comparison of the sheets will then help in evaluating progress in the areas focused upon as well as others, and in identifying areas which need additional prayer and attention.

b. **Worksheets for each character trait** from the SPIRITUAL PROGRESS EVALUATION WORKSHEET. On page 127, an additional worksheet is provided to use to make photocopies for the forty-five areas of godliness. [Or, extra sheets can be purchased from the publisher.] From this page a copy can be made for each of the forty-five topics. Each page will then provide a convenient format for recording the most important passage(s) for the particular topic, for meditation and memorization; for comments as needed to help in understanding the teaching; and for notes and to help in forming an "action plan" for putting the teaching into practice.

NOTE: It is important in the evaluation process to try to identify *tangible* evidence of the growth in life. In other words, identify *specific visible changes* in the person that would accompany God's work of grace, or *specific actions* performed by the person which would be a picture in the real world of the trait desired. This is a way to connect the work of grace in the heart with the changed life in the world.

3. **PLAN.**

How do we use the SPIRITUAL PROGRESS EVALUATION WORKSHEET? The following is the recommended approach to using this discipleship tool:

a. **Focus on one character area each week.** First, we will spend an entire week focusing on each particular area, one area each week, moving through the list in order from number 1 through number 45. This way, we will begin to "master" all of the forty-five traits in about a year's time. We will use the Worksheets to guide us in working through each of the weekly character traits.

b. **Pray every day as a family or individual.** In addition to focusing on one character trait per week, we will commit ourselves to the discipline of offering prayer every day for the character areas during our individual or family Meeting Times with the Lord. Each day we will pray for the Lord's grace for one of the areas, moving through the list in order. This way, we will have prayed for all of the areas after about a month and a half's time. Then we will go back to the beginning, and begin again to move through the list, praying for one each day. Then, we will repeat this process over and over again. In doing this, we will constantly keep all the character traits in mind, and continually bathe them in prayer. Also, we will give some attention to *all* of the traits during the first month and a half of our process, and continue to do so after that, without having to wait many months before giving any attention at all to the traits that appear later on the list. All of the traits are very important in the Christian life, and so, while focusing in depth on one particular trait during a week long study, we will also keep the other traits before us, as well.

A WORD ABOUT THE WEEKLY INSTALLMENTS. As we mentioned above, the sequence of this list is accomplished in weekly installments. Just as the Christian life is divided up according to the time between Sabbaths, so we dedicate one week to mastering the teaching of the Word of God in each area. On Sunday afternoon or Monday morning, the topic will be introduced, and through the week Scripture passages will be read and meditated upon, and a chosen passage or two memorized, brief teaching will be received, and prayer will be offered. We will focus on the Scripture passages themselves. On each subsequent day during the week, we will add to the foundation, until an adequate understanding of the teaching is grasped. Before the week is out, a strategy will be adopted for the practice of the teaching in life, noting specific difficulties and hurdles to overcome before success will be achieved. Depending on the area, there may be a place to record successes and failures in obedience to the Word. Then, on the following Sunday, after the "work" of the week in finished, we "rest" in God's sufficiency and celebrate His work in us during the past week in our labor to advance in godliness. We will at that time note the special accomplishments that He has made in our lives by His grace, and we will look forward to His future grace for the following week's work. We will also sign a promise to be faithful in continuing to wholeheartedly strive toward obedience in that area of godliness, and to continue in looking to the Lord for His grace.

NOTE: *By the end of the week, the goal is to master the TEACHING of the principle, but not necessarily to master the principle yet IN LIFE. This is not to say that each teaching of the principle will not be accompanied by actual practice of the principle. On the contrary, the practice of each principle will immediately begin upon receiving the teaching of that principle. The person is responsible for obedience to the Word as soon as that person receives it. But, the principle may not be mastered in life until after some time has passed, after much prayer and discipline. And, perfect performance may never be achieved in this life. What we are aiming at is mastering the teaching, and putting it into practice by faith, while looking to God and His enabling power for the performance of holy principles. The goal is to form a habit of faithful obedience, and to perform that obedience by faith in God's grace.*

A Word to Families: As you ponder the use of this discipleship tool, consider the value of *going through the process together as a family.* In other words, start together at the beginning, and encourage all family members to devote themselves to the same character trait during the same time. Understandably, there may be a huge variation in the depth of spiritual maturity among the different individuals in a family. But God's design is that the older in the faith be involved with the younger, and that there be mutual encouragement and assistance. Also, even the most advanced of Christians have to return again to the foundation from time to time, to renew and perfect graces that may have been present in their lives for many years. Also, as everyone in the family is focused on one aspect of the spiritual life, that teaching can actually be worked on in the day-to-day struggles and relationships in the home. The home then truly becomes an environment for nurturing growth in the tender plant of the Christian faith and life. Finally, if the members of the family are praying for each other for the grace necessary for vital obedience and conformity to the Word, and are constantly encouraging one another in the daily practice of the principles, there can be great hope that much progress will be made in grace and holiness. Indeed, this is God's plan for life and support in the context of the family! ◇

THURSDAY

A STRATEGY: Both of the Worksheets should be dated, and should be used to assist in observing ongoing progress of the person being evaluated. A good doctor would always want a follow-up examination to evaluate the progress of any treatment which has been applied over time. The medication may need to be changed if needed, or additional medication prescribed, or other changes may be necessary. If full recovery has been attained, the patient may be removed from a particular regimen. Of course, in spiritual matters, a behavior may be changed while the heart remains untouched. Care should be taken to continually devote these matters to prayer. The goal is a spiritual renovation of

the heart. In many aspects of spiritual growth, evaluation is difficult and perfection will never be attained in this life. We can, however, note conspicuous progress and pray for still more.

It is recommended that the SPIRITUAL PROGRESS EVALUATION WORKSHEET be filled out once every six months or so, and compared to the previously filled out sheets. The important thing is that this sheet help parents and children in being *purposeful and systematic* in character growth.

The SPIRITUAL INVENTORY WORKSHEET, which we considered last week, is different, in the sense that many characteristics may be part of the continuing personality or temperament of the person. There may not be a need to fill it out again for a while, unless major changes occur in the child which necessitate a restatement of strengths and weaknesses and change in prayer focus. Also, a parent may come to the conclusion that an observation made and recorded was not accurate, or needs to be corrected or amended. Of course, this sheet should be consulted often, for prayer and training.

We have now completed the EXPLANATION part of our studies.

The rest of today, Friday and Saturday. We will now begin, and will continue through tomorrow and Saturday, going through the forty-five areas of godliness on the SPIRITUAL PROGRESS EVALUATION WORKSHEET. During this time, you will familiarize yourself with the Scriptures, and begin thinking about practical ways to teach and implement these traits in life. *Review traits 1-12 today, review traits 13-28 tomorrow, and review traits 29-45 on Saturday.*

The complete SPIRITUAL PROGRESS EVALUATION WORKSHEET is on pages 122 and 123. It is recommended that you look up the passages in your Bible during these days. *For your quick reference, though, the verses are printed out on pages 130 through 136 of this book.* You will need to learn all you can about each passage as the evaluation process proceeds, so that you accurately understand the Scripture and can teach your children its true meaning. [**NOTE:** A good, concise, accurate Commentary on the whole Bible is *Matthew Henry's Commentary* (a number of editions are available widely; check your local Christian bookstore). PICTURES OF LIFE PUBLISHERS plans in the near future to publish individual worksheets for each of the forty-five topics, including brief commentaries on each Scripture passage and practical tips for their teaching an application to life.]

After you familiarize yourself with the forty-five traits, you will make your initial evaluation by filling out a SPIRITUAL PROGRESS EVALUATION WORK-SHEET for each person. Once again, you may photocopy as many copies of the worksheets as you need for your immediate family, or you may purchase additional copies from this publisher.

Dear Stephanie,

It seems so easy lately to focus on the _negative_ in child-rearing, doesn't it? "Don't do this, and don't enjoy that." What about the _positive_? We should be interested in progress, and not just remedy. It is easy to think well of our children when they resolve to avoid sin. And, it is crucial that they so resolve! But do we think often of the fact that the Christian life is not just a negative renouncing of sin, but a positive love of God and righteousness? If our children aren't lead to _prefer_ godliness, all is lost! If they don't _love_ the truth, then when the restraints under our roof that regulate their behavior are removed, they will revert to the _true_ preferences of their hearts. I've seen that happen more than once, in good, faithful, "leader-type" families. As soon as the son or daughter leaves home for college or a job in Alaska, "all hell breaks loose" (so to speak).

What is the _real_ goal of our child-rearing? That we "hear" that our children are walking in the truth? This "_hearing_" implies that the children aren't under our noses at the moment. And, they won't walk in the truth when they are out of our sight, unless they have come to love the _Lord_ of that truth!

KEITH

What is the substance of this goal? Often we think of our goal in terms of intellectual competence and success. Remember, Steph, when the physician came to talk with us after Christopher was born, and told us that our new baby had Down Syndrome? I sat there stunned, and looked at you. Could this be true? You, however, had prepared for this beforehand in prayer. Though we had no knowledge in advance that our baby had Down Syndrome, God had somehow put it in your heart that our child might have that particular condition. You were not surprised when we were told. And the God of our theology held you. Your only response to that doctor's news, without tears or a look of disappointment at all, was to ask, "What can we do for Christopher?"

"Wow!" _I_ thought. "Down Syndrome!" "Well!" _you_ thought. "If the Lord wills this, it must be _fine_!" (So much for the "superior

CHRISTOPHER

spirituality" of _this_ pastor!)
Thankfully, I came to share your
conclusion, and our theology steered _me_
in the right direction, as well (it just
took me hours on our living room couch
with the Lord, later that night . . .),
and I also embraced the Lord's gift.
And, we have never seen Christopher
as a "tragedy" at all! Quite the
opposite, but that's another book . . . .

Why is the challenge of Down Syndrome sometimes seen as such
a tragedy? If our passion is that our children would love and glorify
God, then Down Syndrome isn't a problem. If our passion is that
our child be great in the eyes of the world, Down Syndrome may be
seen as a tragedy. It's interesting, but several Christians tried to
convince me when Christopher was born that this _was_ a tragedy.
Parents want their children to be all they can be, I was told. But,
as you have said, Steph, "Christopher lacks nothing that he needs to
glorify God in just the way that _He_ has planned!" (Even more
severely challenged children glorify God in just the way He has
planned for them to do so, though our nearsighted eyes often have
trouble perceiving it.) Perhaps Christopher won't make a name for
himself, and probably won't pass the bar or earn a PhD. But he
will do what is best: Exalt God's Name! Christopher will be able to
succeed, by God's grace, with all the resources that God has given to
him for _His_ glory. And, that's all that matters. Right?

If our goal is to glorify God, then Christopher can compete on an
even playing field with the best of them!! If anything, he has an
advantage in the pursuit of _godliness_, because of his naturally
humble, sweet, content disposition. And therefore, our goal in
Chris's life is just as attainable as our goal in Keith's, Melissa's,
and Teresa's lives!

Love, Tim

SPIRITUAL PROGRESS EVALUATION

NAME:_____ AGE:_____ DATE:_____

PART I: GENERAL

1. **Is faithful in Personal Meeting Time with God.** (Psalm 5:3, 88:9, 142:5)

1	2	3	4	5	6	7	8	9	10

2. **Loves and fears God.** (Matthew 22:37-38; Deuteronomy 4:10; Joshua 24:14)

1	2	3	4	5	6	7	8	9	10

3. **Honors and obeys parents.** (Exodus 20:12; Ephesians 6:1; Colossians 3:20)

1	2	3	4	5	6	7	8	9	10

4. **Loves neighbor as self; is devoted to fellow-Christians.** (Matthew 22:39; Romans 12:10)

1	2	3	4	5	6	7	8	9	10

5. **Obeys God's Word.** (Isaiah 66:2; Matthew 7:24-27, 28:19-20; James 1:22-25)

1	2	3	4	5	6	7	8	9	10

6. **Desires spiritual pleasures & treasures.** (Ps. 73:25; Matt. 6:19-21; Eph. 5:10; Col. 3:1-3)

1	2	3	4	5	6	7	8	9	10

7. **Is being weaned from love for this world.** (Psalm 73:25; John 12:25; 1 John 2:15-17)

1	2	3	4	5	6	7	8	9	10

8. **Uses time profitably.** (Proverbs 27:1; Ephesians 5:15-16)

1	2	3	4	5	6	7	8	9	10

9. **Shows humility.** (Philippians 2:5-11)

1	2	3	4	5	6	7	8	9	10

10. **Is pure in heart.** (Matthew 5:8)

1	2	3	4	5	6	7	8	9	10

11. **Is generous in giving.** (2 Corinthians 8:1-7)

1	2	3	4	5	6	7	8	9	10

12. **Lets light shine before people in good works.** (Matthew 5:14-16)

1	2	3	4	5	6	7	8	9	10

PART II: THE FRUIT OF THE SPIRIT

13. **Is loving.** (Galatians 5:22)

1	2	3	4	5	6	7	8	9	10

14. **Is joyous.** (Galatians 5:22)

1	2	3	4	5	6	7	8	9	10

15. **Is peaceful.** (Galatians 5:22)

1	2	3	4	5	6	7	8	9	10

16. **Is patient.** (Galatians 5:22; Ephesians 4:2; Colossians 3:12)

1	2	3	4	5	6	7	8	9	10

17. **Is kind and compassionate.** (Gal. 5:22, 23; Eph. 4:2; 32; Col. 3:12; 1 Thess. 5:15; 1 Pet. 3:8)

1	2	3	4	5	6	7	8	9	10

18. **Is good.** (Galatians 5:22)

1	2	3	4	5	6	7	8	9	10

19. **Is faithful.** (Galatians 5:22)

1	2	3	4	5	6	7	8	9	10

20. **Is gentle.** (Galatians 5:23; Ephesians 4:2; Colossians 3:12)

1	2	3	4	5	6	7	8	9	10

21. **Exercises self-control.** (Galatians 5:23)

1	2	3	4	5	6	7	8	9	10

PART III: RELATIONSHIPS AND RESPONSIBILITIES

22. Guards his tongue. (James 1:26, 3:5-10; Matthew 5:22, 12:34-37; Psalm 34:12-13; 1 Peter 3:10)
1	2	3	4	5	6	7	8	9	10

23. No unwholesome talk comes out of his mouth, but builds others up. (Ephesians 4:29)
1	2	3	4	5	6	7	8	9	10

24. Forgives others. (Matthew 6:12, 14-15, 18:21-35; Mark 11:25; Ephesians 4:32; Colossians 3:13)
1	2	3	4	5	6	7	8	9	10

25. Does not repay evil for evil. (Romans 12:17, 19; 1 Thessalonians 5:15; 1 Peter 3:8-9)
1	2	3	4	5	6	7	8	9	10

26. Loves enemies. (Matthew 5:44; Luke 6:28)
1	2	3	4	5	6	7	8	9	10

27. Does everything without complaining or arguing. (Philippians 2:14)
1	2	3	4	5	6	7	8	9	10

28. Lives at peace with others. (Romans 12:18; 1 Thessalonians 5:13)
1	2	3	4	5	6	7	8	9	10

29. Does not show anger, rage, malice. (Colossians 3:8)
1	2	3	4	5	6	7	8	9	10

30. Does not pass judgment on others. (Romans 14:13; James 4:11)
1	2	3	4	5	6	7	8	9	10

31. Rejoices with those who rejoice; mourns with those who mourn. (Romans 12:15)
1	2	3	4	5	6	7	8	9	10

32. Is considerate of others. (Titus 3:2)
1	2	3	4	5	6	7	8	9	10

33. Carries others' burdens. (Galatians 6:2)
1	2	3	4	5	6	7	8	9	10

34. Uses his spiritual gift to serve others. (1 Peter 4:10)
1	2	3	4	5	6	7	8	9	10

35. Shares with those in need. (Romans 12:13)
1	2	3	4	5	6	7	8	9	10

36. Encourages others daily; spurs others on toward love & good deeds. (Heb 3:13, 10:24-25)
1	2	3	4	5	6	7	8	9	10

37. Is humble, not conceited. (Eph 4:2; Col 3:12; Titus 3:2; 1 Pet 3:8, 5:5; Rom 12:16; Gal 5:26)
1	2	3	4	5	6	7	8	9	10

38. Is submissive. (Ephesians 5:21; 1 Peter 5:5)
1	2	3	4	5	6	7	8	9	10

39. Does not grumble against others. (James 5:9)
1	2	3	4	5	6	7	8	9	10

40. Honors others above self. (Romans 12:10; Philippians 2:3)
1	2	3	4	5	6	7	8	9	10

41. Bears with others in love. (Ephesians 4:2; Colossians 3:13)
1	2	3	4	5	6	7	8	9	10

42. Restores gently those caught in sin. (Galatians 6:1)
1	2	3	4	5	6	7	8	9	10

43. Lives in harmony with others. (Romans 12:16; 1 Peter 3:8)
1	2	3	4	5	6	7	8	9	10

44. Does not slander. (Colossians 3:8; Titus 3:2; James 4:11)
1	2	3	4	5	6	7	8	9	10

45. Does not lie; speaks truthfully. (Colossians 3:9; Ephesians 4:25)
1	2	3	4	5	6	7	8	9	10

Personal Meeting Time:

THE WORD

The Word Preached / Taught

Scripture Reading

Personal Reading / Study

SUNDAY

Sermon / teaching:

Scripture reading:

Personal reading / study:

Items for Prayer

MONDAY

Scripture reading: John 14:21, 17:24; 1 Pet 2:2-3; 2 Cor 1:22, 5:5; Eph 1:14; 1 Cor 13:10-11; Phil 3:13-15

Personal reading / study:

Items for Prayer

TUESDAY

Scripture reading: Continue meditating on Monday's passages

Personal reading / study:

Items for Prayer

WEDNESDAY

Scripture reading: Continue meditating on Monday's passages

Personal reading / study:

Items for Prayer

THURSDAY

Scripture reading: Scriptures from character traits

Personal reading / study:

Items for Prayer

FRIDAY

Scripture reading: Scriptures from character traits

Personal reading / study:

Items for Prayer

SATURDAY

Scripture reading: Scriptures from character traits

Personal reading / study:

Items for Prayer

WEEK 5 - SUMMARY SHEET
GUIDING QUESTIONS

[**Note:** *These questions, which are to be answered in the spaces below, are to guide you in reflecting on each day's content. **All** of the questions will not be answered **every** day, but only those that are helpful in processing a particular day's material.*]

1. In what specific ways has my thinking and practice been challenged or transformed by my interaction with today's biblical teaching? What particular teaching will require further study and reflection?
2. For what specific wrong thinking, sinful priorities, or areas of neglect in my responsibility, must I make confession and seek the forgiveness of the Lord?
3. Seeing that I am now responsible to strive to make the Word I have received today a reality in my life, what specifically must I do in response to God? How specifically will my life and relationships be different as a result of my time with God today? What vows might I make to the Lord this Sunday regarding my intentions to be faithful to Him in particular areas? And, seeing that, in order for this life change to become a reality, God must powerfully work by His grace and through His Spirit in my life, what specifically must I ask God to do or provide?
4. Upon what particular Bible verses will I meditate throughout the day? What verses do I desire to post in a conspicuous place to remind me to meditate upon them? What verses will I commit to memory?

MONDAY

TUESDAY

WEDNESDAY

THURSDAY

FRIDAY

SATURDAY

WEEKLY WORKSHEET

Character Trait: **Week of:**

Scripture Passages:

Interpretation / Comments:

Specific Evidence of Grace for which we pray, and for which we look in life (*What **specific visible changes** do we aim toward? What **specific actions** can be performed? What types of things will be **tangible evidence** of growth in grace in this area?*)**:**

"In dependence on God's grace through faith, I promise to be faithful in continuing to wholeheartedly strive toward obedience in this area of godliness." (Place signatures in this box)

IN CONCLUSION . . .

Go for joy! What can be said in conclusion? First, in the way of encouragement, I would sum up the substance of this book like this: Hear from God about the task of prayer, then *go for joy!* Do you think this way about the lifelong endeavor of prayer for your children? Do you count it all joy?

Go for broke! If there is no greater joy in this life than seeing your children walking in the truth, then you would be foolish not to pursue that joy with all you've got. Spare no effort or expense to obtain this joy. Set out to maximize your joy in seeing God's richest blessing come upon your children. This is worth any effort or sacrifice.

"Go fishing!" On the back cover of this book, the question is asked, "Can a busy parent really find depth and richness in this endeavor?" Hopefully, this book has been a useful tool in helping you to do just that. But now it's up to you. Here in Florida, an old fisherman who used to give the daily fishing report for the local TV news, always said, "If you're too busy to go fishing, you're *too busy!*" Though I'm afraid I don't consider fishing to be as high a priority as he apparently did, if we slightly alter his meaning, we can come up with a pretty good slogan for Christian parents: "If you're too busy to *pray*, you're too busy!"

Can *you*, as a busy parent, build (or *continue*) a rewarding and satisfying prayer life for your children? Or are you just too busy? I really believe that it is simply a matter of *priorities*. We find time to do what's important to us. Can we all relate to that? If other things (even *good* things!) crowd prayer out of your life, you're too busy. If prayer is a high enough priority for you, you *will* make time for it, by streamlining your schedule, being ruthless with those good, though less vital, things. In fact, you will build your schedule *around* this, the highest of priorities.

Go for God! God, and fellowship with Him, is what your children need. God is not merely the *key* to happiness and joy. He *is* our happiness and joy. He is most glorified when His people find their deepest delight and satisfaction *in Him*.

So often, when Christians pray for what they think will make their children happy, they forget this simple point. Many things can make this life sweet and enjoyable and successful. But what do we and our children *really* need for joy? This passage from Jeremiah has had a profound effect on my thinking about the Christian life:

Jeremiah 2:11-13 "Has a nation ever changed its gods? (Yet they are not gods at all.)
    But my people have exchanged their Glory for worthless idols.
"Be appalled at this, O heavens, and shudder with great horror," declares the LORD.
"My people have committed two sins: They have forsaken me, the spring of living water,
    and have dug their own cisterns, broken cisterns that cannot hold water." (NIV)

Water is a picture of life and happiness, and God is to be a Fountain of living water to us. But what have we done? Instead of going to Him and drinking freely from His infinite resources to our heart's deepest satisfaction, we have turned away to build our own "containers." What are

these containers, or cisterns? They are anything other than God to which we look to sustain our life, or to satisfy the needs of our heart, or to provide happiness or security. When these "cisterns" that we have built fail us, we are filled with grief and suffering. What do we do? So often, we ask God to "fix" them! In other words, when the things of this world cease to satisfy, or our happiness dries up, or when our world crumbles around us, we cry out to God. But instead of seeing that the things of this world will fail us, and can never satisfy, and then turning to the only One Who CAN satisfy, we ask Him to repair our poor substitutes for Himself in our lives. That seems to be the bulk of much prayer in the church today. "God, please fix this broken cistern! Then I will be restored." But, as the passage implies, we must give up our obstinate belief that what we *really* need is for those cisterns to be functioning. Rather, we need God Himself, and a relationship of love with Him, and an enjoyment of the spiritual sight of His wonderful glory.

Of course, God is glorified also when He mercifully deals with our broken cisterns in response to our cries to Him. But the real message when our world breaks apart is that *we need to return to our God!* We must *fly to the Fountain for relief!* If we are to drink from these living waters to our heart's content, and lead our children to the same Fountain, then we MUST turn from our man-made idols to Him.

Keep going! We come from a generation of Christians that has been taught that you're supposed to be able to write down in your prayer book every day God's answers to your prayers for that day. While this popular practice does emphasize the biblical fact that God does indeed answer prayer, it should be balanced by the fact that God's answers to our prayers aren't always perceived by our weak spiritual "vision," and aren't according to our time table. We can't see all of what God is doing in response to our prayers, and, as the saying goes, "The harvest is at the end of the age, not at the end of the meeting!" Prayer is *waiting* for God.

Lamentations 3:25 The LORD is good to those who wait for Him, to the person who seeks Him.

Since this is true, we must persevere in our prayer. God will bless those who continue steadfastly until He answers in His own way and in His own time.

So, now that you have read this book, what will be the result? If PRAYER FOR MY CHILD has been used in your life by the Lord in establishing a regular habit of purposeful, focused, powerful, impassioned parental prayer, or in transforming your thinking and acting, or in encouraging you in your continuing fight of faith in prayer, or in challenging you toward greater faithfulness in your prayer life, then I will consider my efforts in writing it abundantly rewarded.

And my joy would increase to overflowing upon hearing that, as a result of *the precious prayer of parents*, a multitude in this rising generation is built up in faith and love, mighty in holiness, passionate in service and sacrifice, burning with heartfelt love for the Name and glory of the living God, and awesome as weapons in the hand of the Spirit, indeed ***walking in the truth!***

APPENDIX

SCRIPTURE PASSAGES FROM THE
SPIRITUAL PROGRESS EVALUATION WORKSHEET

1. Is faithful in Personal Meeting Time with God.

Psalm 5:3 In the morning, O LORD, you hear my voice; in the morning I lay my requests before you and wait in expectation. (NIV)

Psalm 88:9 My eyes are dim with grief. I call to you, O LORD, every day; I spread out my hands to you. (NIV)

Psalm 142:5 I cry to you, O LORD; I say, "You are my refuge, my portion in the land of the living." (NIV)

2. Loves and fears God.

Matthew 22:37-38 And He said to him, "'YOU SHALL LOVE THE LORD your God with all your heart, and with all your soul, and WITH ALL YOUR MIND.' This is the great and foremost commandment."

Deuteronomy 4:10 "Remember the day you stood before the LORD your God at Horeb, when the LORD said to me, 'Assemble the people to Me, that I may let them hear My words so they may learn to fear Me all the days they live on the earth, and that they may teach their children.'"

Joshua 24:14 "Now, therefore, fear the LORD and serve Him in sincerity and truth; and put away the gods which your fathers served beyond the River and in Egypt, and serve the LORD."

3. Honors and obeys parents.

Exodus 20:12 "Honor your father and your mother, that your days may be prolonged in the land which the LORD your God gives you."

Ephesians 6:1 Children, obey your parents in the Lord, for this is right.

Colossians 3:20 Children, be obedient to your parents in all things, for this is well-pleasing to the Lord.

4. Loves neighbor as self; is devoted to fellow-Christians.

Matthew 22:39 "The second is like it, 'YOU SHALL LOVE YOUR NEIGHBOR AS YOURSELF.'"

Romans 12:10 Be devoted to one another in brotherly love; give preference to one another in honor.

5. Obeys God's Word.

Isaiah 66:2 "Has not my hand made all these things, and so they came into being?" declares the LORD. "This is the one I esteem: he who is humble and contrite in spirit, and trembles at my word." (NIV)

Matthew 7:24-27 "Therefore everyone who hears these words of Mine, and acts upon them, may be compared to a wise man, who built his house upon the rock. And the rain descended, and the floods came, and the winds blew, and burst against that house; and yet it did not fall, for it had been founded upon the rock. And everyone who hears these words of Mine, and does not act upon them, will be like a foolish man, who built his house upon the sand. And the rain descended, and the floods came, and the winds blew, and burst against that house; and it fell, and great was its fall."

Matthew 28:19-20 "Go therefore and make disciples of all the nations, baptizing them in the name of the Father and the Son and the Holy Spirit, teaching them to observe all that I commanded you; and lo, I am with you always, even to the end of the age."

James 1:22-25 But prove yourselves doers of the word, and not merely hearers who delude themselves. For if anyone is a hearer of the word and not a doer, he is like a man who looks at his natural face in a mirror; for once he has looked at himself and gone away, he has immediately forgotten what kind of person he was. But one who looks intently at the perfect law, the law of liberty, and abides by it, not having become a forgetful hearer but an effectual doer, this man shall be blessed in what he does.

6. Desires spiritual pleasures & treasures.

Psalm 73:25 Whom have I in heaven but you? And earth has nothing I desire besides you. (NIV)

Matthew 6:19-21 "Do not lay up for yourselves treasures upon earth, where moth and rust destroy, and where thieves break in and steal. But lay up for yourselves treasures in heaven, where neither moth nor rust destroys, and where thieves do not break in or steal; for where your treasure is, there will your heart be also."

Ephesians 5:10 Trying to learn what is pleasing to the Lord.

Colossians 3:1-3 If then you have been raised up with Christ, keep seeking the things above, where Christ is, seated at the right hand of God. Set your mind on the things above, not on the things that are on earth. For you have died and your life is hidden with Christ in God.

7. Is being weaned from love for this world.

Psalm 73:25 Whom have I in heaven but you? And earth has nothing I desire besides you. (NIV)

John 12:25 "He who loves his life loses it; and he who hates his life in this world shall keep it to life eternal."

1 John 2:15-17 Do not love the world, nor the things in the world. If anyone loves the world, the love of the Father is not in him. For all that is in the world, the lust of the flesh and the lust of the eyes and the boastful pride of life, is not from the Father, but is from the world. And the world is passing away, and also its lusts; but the one who does the will of God abides forever.

8. Uses time profitably.

Proverbs 27:1 Do not boast about tomorrow, for you do not know what a day may bring forth.

Ephesians 5:15-16 Therefore be careful how you walk, not as unwise men, but as wise, making the most of your time, because the days are evil.

9. Shows humility.

Philippians 2:5-11 Have this attitude in yourselves which was also in Christ Jesus, who, although He existed in the form of God, did not regard equality with God a thing to be grasped, but emptied Himself, taking the form of a bond-servant, and being made in the likeness of men. And being found in appearance as a man, He humbled Himself by becoming obedient to the point of death, even death on a cross. Therefore also God highly exalted Him, and bestowed on Him the name which is above every name, that at the name of Jesus EVERY KNEE SHOULD BOW, of those who are in heaven, and on earth, and under the earth, and that every tongue should confess that Jesus Christ is Lord, to the glory of God the Father.

10. Is pure in heart.

Psalm 73:1 Surely God is good to Israel, to those who are pure in heart. (NIV)

Matthew 5:8 "Blessed are the pure in heart, for they shall see God."

11. Is generous in giving.

2 Corinthians 8:1-7 Now, brethren, we wish to make known to you the grace of God which has been given in the churches of Macedonia, that in a great ordeal of affliction their abundance of joy and their deep poverty overflowed in the wealth of their liberality. For I testify that according to their ability, and beyond their ability they gave of their own accord, begging us with much entreaty for the favor of participation in the support of the saints, and this, not as we had expected, but they first gave themselves to

the Lord and to us by the will of God. Consequently we urged Titus that as he had previously made a beginning, so he would also complete in you this gracious work as well. But just as you abound in everything, in faith and utterance and knowledge and in all earnestness and in the love we inspired in you, see that you abound in this gracious work also.

12. Lets light shine before people in good works.

Matthew 5:14-16 "You are the light of the world. A city set on a hill cannot be hidden. Nor do men light a lamp, and put it under the peck-measure, but on the lampstand; and it gives light to all who are in the house. Let your light shine before men in such a way that they may see your good works, and glorify your Father who is in heaven."

13. Is loving.

Galatians 5:22 But the fruit of the Spirit is love, joy, peace, patience, kindness, goodness, faithfulness...

14. Is joyous.

Galatians 5:22 But the fruit of the Spirit is love, joy, peace, patience, kindness, goodness, faithfulness...

15. Is peaceful.

Galatians 5:22 But the fruit of the Spirit is love, joy, peace, patience, kindness, goodness, faithfulness...

16. Is patient.

Galatians 5:22 But the fruit of the Spirit is love, joy, peace, patience, kindness, goodness, faithfulness...
Ephesians 4:2 With all humility and gentleness, with patience, showing forbearance to one another in love.
Colossians 3:12   And so, as those who have been chosen of God, holy and beloved, put on a heart of compassion, kindness, humility, gentleness and patience.

17. Is kind and compassionate.

Galatians 5:22-23 But the fruit of the Spirit is love, joy, peace, patience, kindness, goodness, faithfulness, gentleness, self-control; against such things there is no law.
Ephesians 4:2 With all humility and gentleness, with patience, showing forbearance to one another in love.
Ephesians 4:32 And be kind to one another, tender-hearted, forgiving each other, just as God in Christ also has forgiven you.
Colossains 3:12 And so, as those who have been chosen of God, holy and beloved, put on a heart of compassion, kindness, humility, gentleness and patience;
1 Thessalonians 5:15 See that no one repays another with evil for evil, but always seek after that which is good for one another and for all men.
1 Peter 3:8 To sum up, let all be harmonious, sympathetic, brotherly, kindhearted, and humble in spirit.

18. Is good.

Galatians 5:22 But the fruit of the Spirit is love, joy, peace, patience, kindness, goodness, faithfulness...

19. Is faithful.

Galatians 5:22   But the fruit of the Spirit is love, joy, peace, patience, kindness, goodness, faithfulness...

20. Is gentle.

Galatians 5:23 ...gentleness, self-control; against such things there is no law.
Ephesians 4:2 With all humility and gentleness, with patience, showing forbearance to one another in love.
Colossians 3:12 And so, as those who have been chosen of God, holy and beloved, put on a heart of compassion, kindness, humility, gentleness and patience.

21. Exercises self-control.

Galatians 5:23 ...gentleness, self-control; against such things there is no law.

22. Guards his tongue.

James 1:26 If anyone thinks himself to be religious, and yet does not bridle his tongue but deceives his own heart, this man's religion is worthless.

James 3:5-10 So also the tongue is a small part of the body, and yet it boasts of great things. Behold, how great a forest is set aflame by such a small fire! And the tongue is a fire, the very world of iniquity; the tongue is set among our members as that which defiles the entire body, and sets on fire the course of our life, and is set on fire by hell. For every species of beasts and birds, of reptiles and creatures of the sea, is tamed, and has been tamed by the human race. But no one can tame the tongue; it is a restless evil and full of deadly poison. With it we bless our Lord and Father; and with it we curse men, who have been made in the likeness of God; from the same mouth come both blessing and cursing. My brethren, these things ought not to be this way.

Matthew 5:22 "But I say to you that everyone who is angry with his brother shall be guilty before the court; and whoever shall say to his brother, 'Raca,' shall be guilty before the supreme court; and whoever shall say, 'You fool,' shall be guilty enough to go into the fiery hell."

Matthew 12:34-37 "You brood of vipers, how can you, being evil, speak what is good? For the mouth speaks out of that which fills the heart. The good man out of his good treasure brings forth what is good; and the evil man out of his evil treasure brings forth what is evil. And I say to you, that every careless word that men shall speak, they shall render account for it in the day of judgment. For by your words you shall be justified, and by your words you shall be condemned."

Psalm 34:12 Who is the man who desires life, and loves length of days that he may see good? Keep your tongue from evil, and your lips from speaking deceit.

1 Peter 3:10 For, LET HIM WHO MEANS TO LOVE LIFE AND SEE GOOD DAYS REFRAIN HIS TONGUE FROM EVIL AND HIS LIPS FROM SPEAKING GUILE.

23. No unwholesome talk comes out of his mouth, but builds others up.

Ephesians 4:29 Let no unwholesome word proceed from your mouth, but only such a word as is good for edification according to the need of the moment, that it may give grace to those who hear.

24. Forgives others.

Matthew 6:12 "And forgive us our debts, as we also have forgiven our debtors."

Matthew 6:14-15 "For if you forgive men for their transgressions, your heavenly Father will also forgive you. But if you do not forgive men, then your Father will not forgive your transgressions."

Matthew 18:21-35 Then Peter came to Jesus and asked, "Lord, how many times shall I forgive my brother when he sins against me? Up to seven times?" Jesus answered, "I tell you, not seven times, but seventy-seven times. Therefore, the kingdom of heaven is like a king who wanted to settle accounts with his servants. As he began the settlement, a man who owed him ten thousand talents was brought to him. Since he was not able to pay, the master ordered that he and his wife and his children and all that he had be sold to repay the debt. The servant fell on his knees before him. 'Be patient with me,' he begged, 'and I will pay back everything.' The servant's master took pity on him, canceled the debt and let him go. But when that servant went out, he found one of his fellow servants who owed him a hundred denarii. He grabbed him and began to choke him. 'Pay back what you owe me!' he demanded. His fellow servant fell to his knees and begged him, 'Be patient with me, and I will pay you back.' But he refused. Instead, he went off and had the man thrown into prison until he could pay the debt. When the other servants saw what had happened, they were greatly distressed and went and told their master everything that had happened. Then the master called the servant in. 'You wicked servant,' he said, 'I canceled all

that debt of yours because you begged me to. Shouldn't you have had mercy on your fellow servant just as I had on you?' In anger his master turned him over to the jailers to be tortured, until he should pay back all he owed. This is how my heavenly Father will treat each of you unless you forgive your brother from your heart."

Mark 11:25 "And whenever you stand praying, forgive, if you have anything against anyone; so that your Father also who is in heaven may forgive you your transgressions."

Ephesians 4:32 And be kind to one another, tender-hearted, forgiving each other, just as God in Christ also has forgiven you.

Colossians 3:13 Bearing with one another, and forgiving each other, whoever has a complaint against anyone; just as the Lord forgave you, so also should you.

25. Does not repay evil for evil.

Romans 12:17 Never pay back evil for evil to anyone. Respect what is right in the sight of all men.

Romans 12:19 Never take your own revenge, beloved, but leave room for the wrath of God, for it is written, "VENGEANCE IS MINE, I WILL REPAY," says the Lord.

1 Thessalonians 5:15 See that no one repays another with evil for evil, but always seek after that which is good for one another and for all men.

1 Peter 3:8-9 To sum up, let all be harmonious, sympathetic, brotherly, kindhearted, and humble in spirit; not returning evil for evil, or insult for insult, but giving a blessing instead; for you were called for the very purpose that you might inherit a blessing.

26. Loves enemies.

Matthew 5:44 "But I say to you, love your enemies, and pray for those who persecute you."

Luke 6:28 Bless those who curse you, pray for those who mistreat you.

27. Does everything without complaining or arguing.

Philippians 2:14 Do all things without grumbling or disputing.

28. Lives at peace with others.

Romans 12:18 If possible, so far as it depends on you, be at peace with all men.

1 Thessalonians 5:13 And that you esteem them [leaders] very highly in love because of their work. Live in peace with one another.

29. Does not show anger, rage, malice.

Colossians 3:8 But now you also, put them all aside: anger, wrath, malice, slander, and abusive speech from your mouth.

30. Does not pass judgment on others.

Romans 14:13 Therefore let us not judge one another anymore, but rather determine this — not to put an obstacle or a stumbling block in a brother's way.

James 4:11 Do not speak against one another, brethren. He who speaks against a brother, or judges his brother, speaks against the law, and judges the law; but if you judge the law, you are not a doer of the law, but a judge of it.

31. Rejoices with those who rejoice; mourns with those who mourn.

Romans 12:15 Rejoice with those who rejoice, and weep with those who weep.

32. Is considerate of others.

Titus 3:2 To malign no one, to be uncontentious, gentle, showing every consideration for all men.

33. Carries others' burdens.

Galatians 6:2 Bear one another's burdens, and thus fulfill the law of Christ.

34. Uses his spiritual gift to serve others.

1 Peter 4:10 As each one has received a special gift, employ it in serving one another, as good stewards of the manifold grace of God.

35. Shares with those in need.

Romans 12:13 Contributing to the needs of the saints, practicing hospitality.

36. Encourages others daily; spurs others on toward love & good deeds.

Hebrews 3:13 But encourage one another day after day, as long as it is still called "Today," lest any one of you be hardened by the deceitfulness of sin.

Hebrews 10:24-25 And let us consider how to stimulate one another to love and good deeds, not forsaking our own assembling together, as is the habit of some, but encouraging one another; and all the more, as you see the day drawing near.

37. Is humble, not conceited.

Ephesians 4:2 With all humility and gentleness, with patience, showing forbearance to one another in love.

Colossians 3:12 And so, as those who have been chosen of God, holy and beloved, put on a heart of compassion, kindness, humility, gentleness and patience.

Titus 3:2 To malign no one, to be uncontentious, gentle, showing every consideration for all men.

1 Peter 3:8 To sum up, let all be harmonious, sympathetic, brotherly, kindhearted, and humble in spirit;

1 Peter 5:5 You younger men, likewise, be subject to your elders; and all of you, clothe yourselves with humility toward one another, for GOD IS OPPOSED TO THE PROUD, BUT GIVES GRACE TO THE HUMBLE.

Romans 12:16 Be of the same mind toward one another; do not be haughty in mind, but associate with the lowly. Do not be wise in your own estimation.

Galatians 5:26 Let us not become boastful, challenging one another, envying one another.

38. Is submissive.

Ephesians 5:21 And be subject to one another in the fear of Christ.

1 Peter 5:5 You younger men, likewise, be subject to your elders; and all of you, clothe yourselves with humility toward one another, for GOD IS OPPOSED TO THE PROUD, BUT GIVES GRACE TO THE HUMBLE.

39. Does not grumble against others.

James 5:9 Do not complain, brethren, against one another, that you yourselves may not be judged; behold, the Judge is standing right at the door.

40. Honors others above self.

Romans 12:10 Be devoted to one another in brotherly love; give preference to one another in honor;

Philippians 2:3 Do nothing from selfishness or empty conceit, but with humility of mind let each of you regard one another as more important than himself.

41. Bears with others in love.

Ephesians 4:2 with all humility and gentleness, with patience, showing forbearance to one another in love.

Colossians 3:13 Bearing with one another, and forgiving each other, whoever has a complaint against anyone; just as the Lord forgave you, so also should you.

42. Restores gently those caught in sin.

Galatians 6:1 Brethren, even if a man is caught in any trespass, you who are spiritual, restore such a one in a spirit of gentleness; each one looking to yourself, lest you too be tempted.

43. Lives in harmony with others.

Romans 12:16 Be of the same mind toward one another; do not be haughty in mind, but associate with the lowly. Do not be wise in your own estimation.

1 Peter 3:8 To sum up, let all be harmonious, sympathetic, brotherly, kindhearted, and humble in spirit.

44. Does not slander.

Colossians 3:8 But now you also, put them all aside: anger, wrath, malice, slander, and abusive speech from your mouth.

Titus 3:2 To malign no one, to be uncontentious, gentle, showing every consideration for all men.

James 4:11 Do not speak against one another, brethren. He who speaks against a brother, or judges his brother, speaks against the law, and judges the law; but if you judge the law, you are not a doer of the law, but a judge of it.

45. Does not lie; speaks truthfully.

Colossians 3:9 Do not lie to one another, since you laid aside the old self with its evil practices,

Ephesians 4:25 Therefore, laying aside falsehood, SPEAK TRUTH, EACH ONE OF YOU, WITH HIS NEIGHBOR, for we are members of one another.

WORKS CITED

Alexander, James W. 1990 [Orig. 1847]. *Thoughts on Family-Worship*. Ligonier, PA: Soli Deo Gloria Publications.

Dedrick, William and Colleen. 1997. *The Little Book of Christian Character and Manners*. Elkton, MD: Holly Hall Publishing.

Gerstner, John. 1990. *Repent or Perish*. Morgan, PA: Soli Deo Gloria.

Edwards, Jonathan. 1974 [Orig. 1834]. *The Works of Jonathan Edwards*. Edinburgh: Banner of Truth.

Edwards, Jonathan. 1972. *The Great Awakening*, ed. C. Goen, *The Works of Jonathan Edwards*. New Haven: Yale University Press.

Machen, J. Gresham. 1984. *The Christian View of Man*. Edinburgh: Banner of Truth.

Piper, John. 1995. *Future Grace*. Sisters, Oregon: Multnomah.

Pratt, Richard L., Jr. *Pray With Your Eyes Open*. Phillipsburg, New Jersey: Presbyterian and Reformed Publishing Company.

Ray, Bruce A. 1978. *Withhold Not Correction*. Phillipsburg, NJ: Presbyterian & Reformed Pub. Co.

Ryle, J. C. 1983. *Train Up A Child In The Way He Should Go* (*The Duties of Parents*). Choteau, MT: Christian Heritage Publisher.

Scougal, Henry. 1986 [Orig. 1795]. *The Life of God in the Soul of Man*. Harrisonburg, VA: Spinkle Publications.

Spurgeon, Charles. 1985. *Spurgeon's Expository Encyclopedia*. Grand Rapids: Baker Book House.

Trumbull, H. Clay. [Orig. 1890]. *Hints on Child Training*. Eugene, Oregon: Great Expectations Book Company.

ABOUT THE SPECIAL SHEETS

SHEETS PROVIDED IN THE FOLLOWING PAGES

The Guide, lists and Covenant from PART ONE. On the following pages you will find copies of various items from the first part of this book. These pages can be cut out from this section for your use in whatever manner you like. Cutting them out from here will allow you to leave intact the copies of the same sheets which are included in the main body of this book. You are encouraged to use these sheets to help you put the teaching of this book into practice. Additional copies of these sheets may be purchased from the publisher.

Here is a list of the sheets included in the following pages, and the location at which they appear in the body of this book:

1. PRAYER FOR MY CHILD guide, from page 15.

2. Additional copies of the PRAYER FOR MY CHILD guide in various abbreviated forms, for cutting out and posting in conspicuous places, using as a book or Bible mark, or carrying in your wallet or purse. These sheets are intended to encourage the parent to pray at various times throughout the day in addition to the morning prayer time. However, you are encouraged to use the *complete* prayer list for your regular prayer time.

3. The Parental Covenant to Pray For My Children prayer requests from page 36.

4. The Parental Covenant to Pray For My Children , from page 37. You may sign the copy of this Covenant which appears on page 37, which will remain in this book, and then also sign the copy in this section to cut out and frame or post in a conspicuous place as a reminder of your Covenant vows.

5. The prayer requests for your child's conversion to Christ from page 50.

SHEETS FOR PHOTOCOPYING BY THE PARENT

The Worksheets from PART TWO. The spiritual evaluation worksheets found in PART TWO will need to be photocopied for your use from the pages on which they appear in this book (if you would prefer having pre-made copies, see below).

SPIRITUAL INVENTORY WORKSHEET. You will need a copy of both pages of this worksheet (pages 106 and 107) for each person in your family. You may want to copy each worksheet so that one page appears on the front and the other page on the back of a single sheet of paper.

SPIRITUAL PROGRESS EVALUATION WORKSHEET.   You will need a copy of this worksheet (pages 122 and 123) for each family member. This worksheet can also go on a single sheet of paper for each person. This second worksheet will have to be filled out again (and again) for each person, perhaps once every six months. The first worksheet may need to be re-done later, as well, if necessary.

SPIRITUAL PROGRESS EVALUATION WEEKLY WORKSHEET.   Finally, you will need one copy of this worksheet (page 127) for your family to use with each of the forty-five traits.

> [NOTE: Please remember that you may photocopy these sheets (as many as you need) *only* for your own immediate family's use. Since these are copyrighted pages, it is a violation of the law (and therefore God's law) to copy pages from this book for your relatives and friends.]

SHEETS AVAILABLE FROM THE PUBLISHER

Parents who desire to purchase printed copies of this book's sheets rather than cutting them out or photocopying them from the book may contact PICTURES OF LIFE PUBLISHERS (for address, see below).

The various copies or packets that are available (prices subject to change):

- The PRAYER FOR MY CHILD Guide in full color, suitable for framing or posting. ($2.95 plus P & H)

- The **Parental Covenant to Pray For My Children** in full color, suitable for framing or posting. In addition to its value in reminding you, whenever you see it, of your solemn commitment to pray, this can be a very effective witness to your children as well as to visitors in your home. ($2.95 plus P & H)

- A packet containing 2 copies of the SPIRITUAL INVENTORY WORKSHEET and 10 copies of the SPIRITUAL PROGRESS EVALUATION WORKSHEET (this packet provides enough sheets for one person). ($1.95 plus P & H)

- A packet containing 50 copies of the SPIRITUAL PROGRESS EVALUATION WEEKLY WORK-SHEET (this packet provides enough worksheets for the 45 character traits, plus 5 extra copies). ($1.95 plus P & H)

- A full-color sheet containing the five copies of the PRAYER FOR MY CHILD Guide in various sizes (half-sized, bookmark, wallet-sized). ($2.95 plus P & H)

PICTURES OF LIFE PUBLISHERS
Mail: P. O. Box 3235, Holiday, FL 34690
e-mail: picturesoflife@aol.com

PRAYER FOR MY CHILD

1. Prayer of giving up this child, and presenting him (or her) to the Lord (1 Samuel 1:11, 22, 27; Genesis 22:2, 12, 15-17; Romans 12:1).

2. Prayer for God's blessing on this child (Num. 6:22-27; Matt. 19:13).

3. Prayer for this child's eternal soul, as though today were the last day of his life (Proverbs 27:1).

4. Prayer for this child's spiritual and physical protection (from spiritual and physical harm, kidnapping, abuse, etc.).

5. Prayer for this child's perseverance in faith throughout his life, for God's continued care for his needs should I not survive to see him grown. Prayer for his future marriage partner, etc.

6. Prayer on behalf of this child for grace for his spiritual life in the following areas:

   -Prayer of confession of specific sins which he has committed, prayer for pardon, and for his spiritual healing and restoration. Confession of my own sins as though they were my child's sins. Prayer for my child concerning tendencies in myself and in my spouse that may be passed on to our child (i.e., depression, abuse, slothfulness, etc.).

   -Prayer for grace for my child to love God with all his heart, soul, mind and strength, and his neighbor as himself (Matthew 22:37-40).

   -Prayer for love for God's Word, for his receiving it with glad obedience (especially those commands which specifically address children, such as honoring and obeying parents).

   -Prayer that God would pour out the Spirit of prayer on my child, so that he might develop a habit of prayer early, to continue for his lifetime.

   -Prayer for grace for my child to increasingly desire spiritual pleasures and treasures, as he seeks his happiness in God, and for weaning from love of the treasures and pleasures of this world.

   -Prayer for grace to protect this child against specific temptations which he is now fighting by faith, and the temptations which he can be expected to fight in the future.

   -Prayer for grace for dealing with present and future suffering and trials, and with his fears and sorrows.

   -Prayer for grace for purity and for humility in his life.

   -Prayer for grace for personal ministry and usefulness (use of spiritual gifts, love in relationships, compassion for the lost, opportunities for service and sharing the gospel, school, job, etc).

   -Prayer for grace to love his enemies, and for a forgiving spirit toward those who persecute or mistreat him (Matthew 5:44; Luke 6:28).

7. Prayer for his physical life and health, and for his material needs.

8. Prayer for specific spiritual needs of this child, from the INVENTORY & EVALUATION sheets.

Prayer for My Child
Key Items

1. Giving this child up to the Lord.
2. God's blessing on this child.
3. Eternal soul.
4. Spiritual and physical protection.
5. Lifelong concerns: perseverance in faith, future spouse, other needs.
6. Grace in these areas:
   - Confession of his specific sins; pardon; healing; restoration. Also, my sins and weaknesses.
   - Love God and neighbor.
   - Love for God's Word and obedience to it.
   - Spirit of prayer.
   - Desire for spiritual pleasures and treasures; weaning from the world.
   - Protection from present and future specific temptations.
   - Grace in present and future suffering and trials.
   - Purity and humility.
   - Personal ministry and usefulness (spiritual gifts, love, compassion, service, witness).
   - Love for enemies and a forgiving spirit.
7. Physical life and health, and material needs.
8. Specific spiritual needs (from evaluation sheets).

NOTE: *This abbreviated form should only be used as a reminder of the list for prayer throughout the day. The full sheet which is included with this book should be used regularly in the parent's prayer time.*

© 1999 Tim A. Spilman

Prayer for My Child
Key Items

1. Giving child up to God.
2. God's blessing.
3. Eternal soul.
4. Spiritual/physical protection.
5. Lifelong: faith, spouse, etc.
6. Grace for:
   - his sins and mine.
   - Love God and neighbor.
   - Love/obey God's Word.
   - Spirit of prayer.
   - Spiritual desires; weaning.
   - Protect from temptations.
   - Grace in suffering/trials.
   - Purity and humility.
   - Personal ministry.
   - Forgiving spirit.
7. Physical life/health/needs.
8. Specific spiritual needs.

© 1999 Tim A. Spilman

Prayer for My Child
Key Items

1. Giving child up to God.
2. God's blessing.
3. Eternal soul.
4. Spiritual/physical protection.
5. Lifelong: faith, spouse, etc.
6. Grace for:
   - his sins and mine.
   - Love God and neighbor.
   - Love/obey God's Word.
   - Spirit of prayer.
   - Spiritual desires; weaning.
   - Protect from temptations.
   - Grace in suffering/trials.
   - Purity and humility.
   - Personal ministry.
   - Forgiving spirit.
7. Physical life/health/needs.
8. Specific spiritual needs.

© 1999 Tim A. Spilman

Prayer for My Child
Key Items

1. Giving child up to God.
2. God's blessing.
3. Eternal soul.
4. Spiritual/physical protection.
5. Lifelong: faith, spouse, etc.
6. Grace for:
   - his sins and mine.
   - Love God and neighbor.
   - Love/obey God's Word.
   - Spirit of prayer.
   - Spiritual desires; weaning.
   - Protect from temptations.
   - Grace in suffering/trials.
   - Purity and humility.
   - Personal ministry.
   - Forgiving spirit.
7. Physical life/health/needs.
8. Specific spiritual needs.

© 1999 Tim A. Spilman

Prayer Requests for the
Parental Covenant to Pray For My Children

Pray for God's special enabling for you to receive whatever He does in your life and in the life of your child. Pray not only that you would accept it, but that you would be prepared and strengthened in your heart to embrace whatever happens as in God's control and part of His good and wise plan for our good and His glory. Pray that you would be satisfied in God's ways, trusting in His goodness.

Pray that God would enable you to release your emotional hold on your child, and give him up to the Lord as a living sacrifice. Entrust the child to the LORD, saying, "I totally trust in Your goodness! Do with this child as You will! Your counter-claim on my child blots out my claim on him! I release my claim! I give him up as though he were DEAD, that You may grant him LIFE; otherwise I'll lose him forever."

Establish the daily discipline of looking to God in prayer, habitually giving up your child to Him, knowing that He can be depended upon to give you grace adequate to cover even the most devastating experience or loss on earth. *"Now to him who is able to do immeasurably more than all we ask or imagine, according to his power that is at work within us..."* (Ephesians 3:20; NIV)

Pray that you would be truly reconciled in your mind and heart to the fact that your child does not belong to you, but to the Lord. Pray that you would be reconciled to the fact that his life and well-being is dependent on God. Reconfirm this thinking every day in your prayer, so that, if God does take your child, you would be prepared for that by His grace.

Pray for God's grace in your responsibility of raising the child for Him. Far from being an abdication of responsibility, giving up the child is rather an act of engaging ourselves in this responsibility. In talking of "giving up" the child, we are talking about giving up the possession of the child, the rights to the child, and the emotional dependence on the child, rather than the responsibility for the child.

Parental Covenant to Pray For My Children

I hereby release each child to my Lord, affirming to Him:

"*I totally trust in Your goodness. Do with this child as You will. Your counter-claim on my child erases my claim on him. I release my claim. I give him up as though he were dead, that You may give him new life that will last forever. I am reconciled in my heart and mind to the fact that my child does not belong to me, but to You, whose love is greater than my own, and that his life and well-being are totally dependent on You. I will look to You daily to bless my child and save him and keep him in Your care. And, as I daily reconfirm this thinking in my prayer, I can trust You so that, if You do take my child from me, I will be prepared by Your grace.*"

*I hereby confirm my responsibility for each child
my Lord has entrusted to my care. By His grace,
I resolve to not be negligent in my responsibility for each child:*

"*I give myself wholly to do whatever I can for his salvation night and day, sacrificing worldly interests and profit for his eternal good. I will not cease to faithfully set before him his danger, and will declare Your whole Word to him. I will not lead this soul into any snare by my ill example. I will not neglect any means that You have appointed to turn him from sin to God. I especially now solemnly commit myself to pray faithfully for my child daily, as I am guided by this prayer list and explanation.*"

Name(s) of child(ren): _____

_____

Parental Signature: _____ Date: _____

Witnesses: _____

PRAYERS FOR CONVERSION

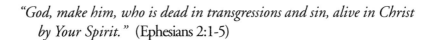

"God, remove from him (or her) that heart of stone and give him a heart of flesh." (Ezekiel 11:19)

"Lord, circumcise his heart, so that he may love you with all his heart and with all his soul, and live." (Deuteronomy 30:6)

"God, make him, who is dead in transgressions and sin, alive in Christ by Your Spirit." (Ephesians 2:1-5)

"Father, let Your light shine in his heart, to give him the light of the knowledge of the glory of God in the face of Christ." (2 Corinthians 4:6)

"Lord, save him through the washing of rebirth and renewal by the Holy Spirit." (Titus 3:5)

"Father, grant him repentance leading him to a knowledge of the truth, that he will come to his senses and escape from the trap of the devil." (2 Timothy 2:25, 26)

"Lord, open his heart to believe and respond to the Gospel." (Acts 16:14)

"Father, put your Spirit in him and move him to follow Your decrees and be careful to keep Your laws." (Ezekiel 36:27)